Mystery Stories

edited by Daniel Barber

Series Editor: Ceri Jones

Macmillan Education
Between Towns Road, Oxford OX4 3PP
A division of Macmillan Publishers Limited
Companies and representatives throughout the world

ISBN 978–0–230–44120–0

All additional material written by Daniel Barber
The authors have asserted their rights to be identified as the authors of these
works in accordance with the Copyright, Design and Patents Act 1988.

Designed by Carolyn Gibson
Cover photographs courtesy of Alamy/Pick and Mix Images (main photo);
Superstock/Fotosearch (inset)

The author and publishers are grateful for permission to reprint the following
copyright material:

Page 81: Story 'The Mildenhall Treasure' taken from *The Wonderful Story of Henry
Sugar*, and *Six More* by Roald Dahl, copyright © Roald Dahl 1988, reprinted by
permission of David Higham Associates, London.

These materials may contain links for third party websites. We have no control
over, and are not responsible for, the contents of such third party websites. Please
use care when accessing them.

Although we have tried to trace and contact copyright holders before publication,
in some cases this has not been possible. If contacted we will be pleased to rectify
any errors or omissions at the earliest opportunity.

Printed and bound in Th...

2019   2018   2017   2(
10   9   8   7   6

Contents

Macmillan Literature Collections

Welcome to the *Macmillan Literature Collections* – a series of advanced level readers containing original, unsimplified short stories written by famous classic and modern writers. We hope that these stories will help to ease the transition from graded readers to reading authentic novels.

Each collection in the series includes:

Introduction

- an introduction to the short story
- tips for reading authentic texts in English
- an introduction to the genre
- a carefully-chosen selection of classic and modern short stories.

The stories

Each story is presented in three parts: the introduction and pre-reading support material; the story; and post-reading activities. Each part includes the following sections:

- *About the author* – in-depth information about the author and their work
- *About the story* – information about the story, including background information about setting and cultural references
- *Summary* – a brief summary of the story that does not give away the ending.

Pre-reading activities

- *Key vocabulary* – a chance to look at some of the more difficult vocabulary related to the main themes and style of the story before reading the story
- *Main themes* – a brief discussion of the main themes, with questions to keep in mind as you read.

The story

You will find numbered footnotes in the stories. These explain cultural and historical references, and key words that you will need to understand the text. Many of these footnotes give definitions of words which are very formal, old-fashioned or rarely used in modern English. You will find more common, useful words and phrases from the stories in the *Glossary* at the end of the book. Words included in the *Glossary* will appear in **bold**.

Post-reading activities

- *Understanding the story* – comprehension questions that will help you make sure you have understood the story
- *Language study* – a section that presents and practises key linguistic and structural features of authentic literary texts (you will find an index of the areas covered at the end of the book)
- *Literary analysis* – discussion questions that guide you to an in-depth appreciation of the story, its structure, its characters and its style.

In addition, at the end of each book there are:
- suggested *Essay questions*
- a comprehensive *Glossary* highlighting useful vocabulary from each story
- an index for the *Language study* section.

How to use these books

You can use these books in whatever way you want. You may want to start from the beginning and work your way through. You may want to pick and choose. The *Contents* page gives a very brief, one-line introduction to each story to help you decide where to start. You may want to learn about the author and the story before you read each one, or you may prefer to read the story first and then find out more about it afterwards. Remember that the stories and exercises can be challenging, so you may want to spend quite a long time studying each one. The most important thing is to enjoy the collection – to enjoy reading, to enjoy the stories and to enjoy the language that has been used to create them.

Answer keys

In many cases you can check your answers in the story by using the page references given. However, an Answer key for all the exercises is available at www.macmillanenglish.com/readers.

Introduction

What is a short story?

A short story is shorter than a novel, but longer than a poem. It is usually between 1,000 and 20,000 words long. It tells a story which can usually be read quite quickly. It often concentrates on one, central event; it has a limited number of characters, and takes place within a short space of time.

History of the short story

Stories and storytelling have existed for as long as people have had language. People love, and need, stories. They help us explain and understand the world. Before people could read or write, story tellers travelled from village to village, telling stories.

The first written stories developed from this storytelling tradition. Two of the best known examples of early, written stories in Europe appeared in the 14th century. Chaucer's *Canterbury Tales* and Bocaccio's *Decameron* are both based on the same idea. A group of people who are travelling or living together for a short time, agree to tell each other stories. Their individual short stories are presented together as one long story.

The first modern short stories appeared at the beginning of the 19th century. Early examples of short story collections include the *Fairy Tales* (1824–26) of the Brothers Grimm, and Edgar Allan Poe's *Tales of the Grotesque and Arabesque* (1840). In the late 19th century, printed magazines and journals became very popular and more and more short stories were published. By the 20th century most well-known magazines included short stories in every issue and the publishers paid a lot of money for them. In 1952 Ernest Hemingway's short story, *The Old Man and the Sea*, helped sell more than five million copies of the magazine *Life* in just two days.

The short story today

Today, short stories are often published in collections called anthologies. They are usually grouped according to a particular category – by theme, topic, national origin, time or author. Some newspapers and magazines continue to print individual stories. Many short stories are first published on the Internet, with authors posting them on special interest websites and in online magazines.

Reading authentic literary texts in English

Reading authentic literary texts can be difficult. They may contain grammatical structures you have not studied, or expressions and sayings you are not familiar with. Unlike graded readers, they have not been written for language students. The words have been chosen to create a particular effect, not because they are easy or difficult. But you do not need to understand every word to understand and enjoy the story. When you are reading in your own language you will often read so quickly that you skip over words, and read for the general effect, rather than the details. Try to do the same when you are reading in English. Remember that stopping to look up every word you don't know slows you down and stops you enjoying the story.

When you are reading authentic short stories, remember:
- It should be a pleasure!
- You should read at your own pace.
- Let the story carry you along – don't worry about looking up every word you don't understand.
- Don't worry about difficult words unless they stop you from understanding the story.
- Try not to use the *Glossary* or a dictionary when you're reading.

You might want to make a note of words to look up later, especially key words that you see several times (see *Using a Dictionary* on page 9 for more tips on looking up and recording new words). But remember, you can always go back again when you have finished the story. That is the beauty of reading short stories – they are short! You can finish one quite quickly, especially if you do not worry about understanding every single word; then you can start again at the beginning and take your time to re-read difficult passages and look up key words.

Preparing yourself for a story

It is always a good idea to prepare yourself, mentally, before starting a story.
- Look at the title. What does it tell you about the story? What do you expect the story to be about?
- If there is a summary, read it. This will help you follow the story.
- Quickly read the first few paragraphs and answer these questions: Where is it set?

When is it set?

Who is the main character?

- As you read, concentrate on following the gist (the general idea) of the story. You can go back and look at the details later. You can use the questions at the end of the story (see *Understanding the story*) to help you make sure you understand what is happening.

Tips for dealing with difficult passages

Some stories include particularly difficult passages. They are usually descriptive and give background information, or set the scene. They are generally difficult to follow because they are full of specific details. Try to read these passages quickly, understanding what you can, and then continue with the story. Make a note of the passage and come back to it later, when you have finished the whole story.

If, at any time, you are finding it difficult to follow the story, go back to this difficult passage. It may hold the answers to your questions.

Read through the passage again carefully and underline all the unknown words. Try to understand as much as you can from the immediate context and what you now know about the story. Then, look up any remaining words in the *Glossary* at the back of the book, or in your dictionary.

Tips for dealing with difficult words

- Decide if the word (or phrase) is important to the overall message. Read the whole paragraph. Do you understand the general meaning? Yes? Then the word isn't important. Don't worry about it. *Keep reading!*
- If you decide the word is important, see if you can work out its meaning from the context. Is it a verb, a noun or an adjective? Is it positive or negative? What word would you translate it into in your language? Underline it or make a note of it and the page number, but *keep reading*. If it really is an important word, you will see it again.
- If you keep seeing the same word in the story, and you still can't understand it, look in your monolingual dictionary!

Using a dictionary

Looking up words

Before you look up the word, look at it again in its context. Decide what part of speech it is. Try to guess its meaning from the context. Now look it up in your dictionary. There may be more than one definition given. Decide which one is the most appropriate. If the word is something very specific, e.g. the name of a flower or tree, you may want to use a bilingual dictionary to give you the exact translation.

Let's look at how this works in practice. Look at this short extract and follow the instructions below.

> ... there is a little valley or rather **lap** of land among high hills, which is one of the quietest places in the whole world. A small **brook** glides through it, with just murmur enough to **lull** one to repose*
>
> *literary: *sleep or rest*
> *The Legend of Sleepy Hollow* by Washington Irvine

1   Look at the words in bold and decide what part of speech they are – noun, verb, adjective, etc.

2   Try to guess what it might mean.

3   Look at the extracts below from the *Macmillan English Dictionary for Advanced Learners*. Choose the most appropriate definition.

Words with more than one entry	**brook¹** noun
Sometimes the same word belongs to more than one word class: for example, **brook** can be both a noun and a verb. Each word class is shown as a separate entry. The small number at the end of the head-word tells you that a word has more than one entry.	a small river
	brook² verb
	not brook – to definitely not allow or accept something.
	lap¹ noun
	1 the top half of your legs above your knees when you sit down.
	2 one complete turn around a course in a race
	PHRASE in the lap of luxury in very comfortable and expensive conditions
Idioms and fixed expressions	**lap²** verb
Some words are often used in idioms and fixed expressions. These are shown at the end of the entry, following the small box that says PHRASE.	1 if an animal laps water, it drinks it gently with its tongue
	lull¹ noun
	a quiet period during a very active or violent situation
	lull² verb
Words with more than one meaning	1 to make someone feel relaxed and confident so that they are not prepared for something unpleasant to happen to lull someone into a false sense of security
Many words have more than one meaning, and each different meaning is shown by a number.	2 to make someone relaxed enough to go to sleep

Dictionary extracts adapted from the Macmillan English Dictionary 2nd Edition/2007 © Macmillan Publishers Limited 2005 *www.macmillandictionary.com*

Keeping a record

When you have looked in your dictionary, decide if the word is interesting or useful to you. If it is, make a note of it, and write down its definition. Make a note of the sentence where you found it in the story, then write one or two more examples of your own. Only do this for those words you think you will need to use in the future.

Here is an example of how you might record the word *lull*.

'with just murmur enough to <u>lull</u> one to repose'
<u>Lull</u> – to make you feel relaxed enough to go to sleep
e.g. The quiet sound of the waves lulled me to sleep
The mother sang to her baby to lull it to sleep

Literary analysis

The *Literary analysis* section is written to encourage you to consider the stories in more depth. This will help you to appreciate them better and develop your analytical skills. This section is particularly useful for those students who are studying, or intending to study, literature in the medium of English. Each section includes literary terms with which you may or may not be familiar.

Macmillan Readers website

For more help with understanding these literary terms, and to find Answer keys to all the exercises and activities, visit the Macmillan Readers website at www.macmillanenglish.com/readers. There you will also find a wealth of resources to help your language learning in English, from listening exercises to articles on academic and creative writing.

The genre of Mystery

What is mystery?

A mystery is something that is kept secret or remains unexplained or unknown. It is a question still unanswered, perhaps unanswerable. We talk about *the mysteries of the universe*, for example, to describe things in nature that we still do not understand. Famous mysteries include unexplained phenomena, missing people, strange creatures and unsolved crimes. The Bermuda triangle is the name given to an area in the Atlantic Ocean where an unusual number of ships and planes have disappeared over the years. Tales of large beasts, such as the Yeti in Nepal and Bigfoot in North America, make up a part of our cultural mythology. Shadowy figures such as Jack the Ripper, the unidentified London murderer of the 19th century, continue to hold their appeal many, many years after the events. All these stories, true and mythical, can be described as mysteries.

Alfred Hitchcock, the famous film director and master of mystery and suspense, provides a suitable definition of mystery in terms of fiction: 'A mystery is something that the public are trying to discover … it's an intellectual process.' When we read or watch a mystery, we are being challenged to explain something about the story that is not obvious or easy to understand.

Why do we like mystery stories?

A sense of mystery in fiction has always appealed to readers. It works on our desire to take on intellectual challenges, to test our intelligence, and we enjoy it when our theories are confirmed or our curiosity is satisfied. There is also a side of us that enjoys not knowing, and some writers refuse to give us the satisfaction of a neat answer to a mystery. Instead they leave us in the dark, allowing the questions to stay with us long after we have finished the story.

We are attracted to the unknowable. Einstein said that 'the most beautiful thing we can experience is the mysterious. It is the source of all true art and science.'

The label *mystery story* means different things to different people. The nature of the mystery differs with each story in this collection and the way the writers deal with mystery varies. Some solve it completely, others leave questions unanswered.

Types of mystery

Puzzles

Two of the stories in this book pose questions for the reader to solve for themselves. Their writers, like many mystery writers, seem to want to play with us and challenge us to think by setting an intellectual puzzle, or game, with questions that we have to answer by thinking carefully.

This type of mystery has a well-established history, going back to popular tales in literature's distant past. In Chaucer's *The Canterbury Tales*, written in the 14th century, 'The Franklin's Tale' ends with a question for its listeners to answer. Many religious stories illustrate moral problems with short stories that require the audience to reflect on or discuss their meaning.

Supernatural mysteries

Unexplained events in real life are a popular source of inspiration for mystery writers, who may choose to explain them logically or via supernatural means. Sir Arthur Conan Doyle, one of whose stories appears in this collection, provides a good example in another tale he wrote which tries to explain the famous disappearance of the entire crew of a ship, the *Mary Celeste*. He invents a rational, although extremely improbable, story to fill in the gaps surrounding the ghost ship's strange last voyage. Countless books and TV dramatizations give their own versions of popular myths, in such formats as *The X Files* and *The Twilight Zone*. In many cases, the explanations for events are supernatural, or ghostly, in nature, or rely on extremely unrealistic phenomena such as aliens and magic powers.

In this sense, then, many horror stories fall under the category of *mystery* as well. (There is a Macmillan Literature Collection devoted to this particular genre, *Horror Stories*).

Psychological mysteries

Sometimes the most interesting mysteries can be found in people's motives and behaviour. In two of the stories in this collection, the mystery exists inside the mind of a central character. The question is: what makes people act in a particular way?

The human mind and its inner workings are a more recent area for literature to explore. An early example is *The Turn of the Screw* by a pioneer of this sub-genre, the American author, Henry James. In it the exact nature of the horror that haunts the main character is never determined. The children in the story seem to be able to see ghosts, but are they real, or are they just in the disturbed mind of the narrator? We never find out. A Hollywood film, *The Sixth Sense*, about a boy who sees dead people, is a good illustration of the sub-genre. Several events take place that the main character cannot understand until he realizes a horrifying truth. *The Sixth Sense* exemplifies how very popular the psychological mystery has become in the last century or so.

Whodunnits

The *mystery* label often refers to stories in which a crime remains unsolved until the main character, a detective who uses his or her intelligence and logic, eventually discovers the criminal's identity. These are known as 'whodunnits' (who-done-it?). The criminal is revealed only at the very end of the story, allowing the reader plenty of time to come up with their own theories and guesses.

Agatha Christie is perhaps the most famous writer of mysteries of this type, and nearly all of her novels star a detective or amateur 'sleuth' who picks up clues through the story and by the end is able to confidently state who the criminal is, how they did it and why. The reader is given the satisfaction of discovering the truth at the end. The mystery has been solved.

(There is a Macmillan Literature Collection devoted to this particular genre, *Crime Stories*.)

Conspiracies

The collection starts with a story by Sir Arthur Conan Doyle, the creator of Sherlock Holmes. In many ways it is a whodunnit, but it can also be considered a political thriller or conspiracy (a secret plan by a group of people to do something bad or illegal).

The assassination in 1963 of the US President John F. Kennedy is perhaps the best-known true news story that has driven people to try to uncover conspiracies behind the crime. Although Conan Doyle's tale of conspiracy is fictional, it has all the makings of a real-life thriller.

If there is one thing that all mystery stories have in common, it is that they ask us to think about what we are reading in a critical way, almost as if we were the detectives ourselves.

The Lost Special

by Sir Arthur Conan Doyle

About the author

Sir Arthur Conan Doyle is best known as the creator of the great fictional detective, Sherlock Holmes. As well as the Sherlock Holmes stories, he also wrote science fiction and horror stories, historical novels, and political pamphlets[1]. He led a full and public life, travelling widely and often, and he was greatly admired and respected in his own lifetime. Throughout his life he was interested in explaining the unexplainable, and finding solutions to all kinds of problems: real life criminal cases, political issues and even the question of whether there is life after death.

Arthur Ignatius Conan Doyle was born in Edinburgh, Scotland, on 22nd May 1859 into a large Catholic family. His mother was Irish. She remained an important figure throughout his life, encouraging him in his writing career. His father was from England, and when he was nine, Arthur was sent away to school there, where he was very unhappy. After finishing school, he studied medicine. In his spare time, he began to write stories, which were published in various magazines.

After serving for a short time as a ship's doctor, he started working in private medical practice, first in Southsea, on the south coast of England, and then later in London. But business was slow, he had very few patients and he had to write stories to supplement his income.

In 1887 his first long work was published, *A Study in Scarlet*. This was the first of several Sherlock Holmes novels. The second, *The Sign of the Four* (1890), was followed by his first short story that featured Sherlock Holmes, *A Scandal in Bohemia* (1891). Other stories soon followed as regular monthly features in *The Strand Magazine*.

During the same period, he also wrote a series of successful historical novels. He soon realized that he could make more money writing than working as a doctor and he decided to write full-time.

However, in 1900, he went to South Africa to work as a field doctor during the Boer War. He wrote an account of the war, *War in South*

1 short books about political or social problems

Africa: Its Cause and Conduct, defending the role of the British forces in South Africa. In the same year he was given a knighthood for his services to his country, and became Sir Arthur Conan Doyle.

In the 1900s he became interested in politics. He stood for parliament twice, but was not elected. He supported the movement for women's rights and wrote a book, *The Crime of the Congo,* describing the horrors in that country. He also investigated two crimes that had already been solved by the police. In both investigations, Conan Doyle discovered that the police had been wrong and, as a result, two innocent men were freed from prison.

Conan Doyle married twice. His first marriage was to Louisa Hawkins, with whom he had two children, Mary and Kingsley. In the 1890s Louisa became very ill and he nursed her for nearly ten years before she died in 1906.

He was married again in 1907, to the much younger Jean Leckie, who he had known for many years. The two travelled to the United States and Europe.

Conan Doyle suffered many tragedies in his personal life, not only with the loss of his first wife, but also during and after the First World War of 1914-1918, when he lost his father, his son, his brother, two nephews and two brothers-in-law. These losses affected him greatly and he became very depressed. He wrote less and spent more time studying spiritualism and scientific research into the existence of life after death. He died of a heart attack in 1930 at the age of 71.

He is remembered for his literary achievements, his character and his public service, and his tombstone reads: 'Steel blue, Blade straight, Arthur Conan Doyle, Knight, patriot, physician and man of letters'.

About the story

The Lost Special was first published in 1898 in *The Strand Magazine,* where many of Conan Doyle's Sherlock Holmes stories had previously been published. Although Holmes is not mentioned by name in the story, it includes a letter printed in *The Times* newspaper written by 'an amateur reasoner of some celebrity', who is assumed to be the great fictional detective. The story later appeared in the 1923 collection, *Tales of Terror and Mystery.*

Background information

The age of steam

At the end of the nineteenth century, people could move from place to place more quickly than they had dreamed of doing just a few decades earlier, thanks to steam power. A system of railways that covered much of the world was integrated with regular ocean crossings on steam-powered ships, or 'steamers'. You could climb aboard an express train in the north of England and arrive in London in just a few hours. It was even possible in those days to hire your own private train, called a 'special', provided you could pay for it, of course. This is what the 'special' referred to in the title is.

The railway was important from a cultural point of view in nineteenth-century Britain. When new lines were opened for the smaller towns and villages, people celebrated with parties and live music. Young boys dreamed of riding in the cabin of a steam engine. Britain had a large empire at that time, with Queen Victoria at its head, and the railway represented the power and modernity of British life to the rest of the world. It was so central to Victorian life that it even affected the way time was perceived. For the first time in ordinary people's lives, an awareness of the exact time became crucial if they didn't want to miss their connection. 'Railway time' became the standard by which clocks were set throughout Britain.

It was not just people who travelled by train; coal and iron was transported on the railways from the ironworks and coal mines (or 'collieries') to the great industrial cities and ports. The mystery of the lost special takes place on and around the main line between Liverpool, in the industrial north of England, and London.

The telegraph

Like people, information was moving faster than ever. Britain stood at the centre of an extensive telecommunications network known as the 'electrical telegraph'. Even though it was only about forty years old, it connected Britain to every corner of its empire and the world. It was the Victorian equivalent of the telephone system. Electrical cables were laid along railway tracks and even under oceans to join stations, cities and continents so that messages, or 'telegrams', could be sent, or 'wired', almost instantaneously. Simple electrical signals were created by a telegraph operator at one end of the line using a special language of long and short sounds called Morse code. An operator many miles away would receive and decode the sounds back into English. Like text messages today, messages had to be short, and special forms of writing known as 'telegraphese' were developed to keep the number of words to a minimum. Examples of telegrams appear in the story.

Summary

It may help you to know something about what happens in the story before you read it. Don't worry, this summary does not tell you how the story ends!

This story concerns the apparently impossible disappearance of a train as it travels from Liverpool to London. It is in the form of a report which is written eight years after the train goes missing. It contains a variety of different texts: letters, a police report, telegrams and a confession. The story teller says that the reason he is summarising the case is to show the facts as clearly as he can.

A foreign gentleman and his assistant arrive at Liverpool railway station and ask to speak to the station superintendent. They have urgent business in Paris and demand a special train to take them to London as soon as possible. The superintendent agrees and organizes a train, which leaves Liverpool at half past four. It is expected in Manchester before six o'clock but a telegram arrives on the superintendent's desk at a quarter past six stating that the special has not arrived there. The superintendent sends telegrams to stations between Liverpool and Manchester and discovers from the replies that the train has disappeared completely. More searching by the local station masters finds no signs of the missing train but they do find the train driver lying dead next to the rail.

Further investigations reveal nothing, and despite the public interest in the mystery, no one can come up with a good explanation. What could possibly have happened to the special train from Liverpool to London?

The case goes cold …

Then, eight years later, the answer to the mystery arrives from a completely unexpected source. A famous murderer waiting to be executed in a prison in southern France has a confession to make. Why reveal the secret so long after the event, and why now?

Pre-reading activities

Key vocabulary

This section will help you familiarize yourself with some of the more specific vocabulary used in the story. You may want to use it to help you before you start reading, or as a revision exercise after you have finished the story.

On the railway

1 **The mystery concerns a missing train and a busy railway line. Look at the words in bold in the sentences below. Which words describe:**

a) trains? b) parts of trains? c) people? d) parts of the railway?

1 He had missed the London **express**. A **special** must be provided.
2 He left the **superintendent's** office and joined his companion.
3 The powerful **engine** was attached to its **tender,** and had two **carriages and** a **guard's van** behind.
4 The **guard** of the train was James McPherson, who had been some years in the service of the company. The **stoker**, William Smith, was new.
5 And yet there is no **siding** between the two stations. The special must have run off the **metals.**
6 We will have a wire from Kenyon or Barton Moss soon to say that they have found her at the bottom of an **embankment.**
7 The reason no one saw the train is that the line runs through a deep **cutting.**
8 There are twelve ironworks and collieries which have **small-gauge lines** which run **trolly-cars** down to the main line.
9 A gang of railway **platelayers** were working along the line.
10 Now it was just a case of completing a junction with the line and arranging the **points** as they had been before.

2 **Match the words in bold in the sentences above with their definitions (a–q) below.**

Words describing trains

a) a privately hired train for one specific journey
b) a train that gets to its destination quickly by not stopping at many stations on the way

Words describing parts of a train

c) the part of the train where the guard travels, usually at the back
d) the part of a train that carries the coal and water for a steam engine
e) the vehicles that are joined together to make a train for passengers (the American word is 'car')
f) the vehicles that are joined together to carry goods such as coal and iron
g) a vehicle that pulls a train which is powered by steam, electricity or diesel

Words describing people

h) someone whose job is to check tickets, announce the stations, and look after the passengers (an old-fashioned British word. The American word is 'conductor')
i) someone on a train whose job is to add coal to the boiler to provide power to the engine
j) someone who lays and repairs railway tracks.
k) someone who is in charge of something, for example a hospital, railway, or school

Words describing parts of the railway

l) the metal tracks of the railway
m) a short railway track connected to a main line
n) railways with narrow rails for smaller trains
o) a sloping wall of earth or stone beside a road, railway or river
p) a section of railway track that moves between two sets of track so that a train can cross from one to the other
q) a passage cut through rock to allow a road or railway to pass through

3 Which of the words above do you think can no longer be used to refer to modern railways or rail travel?

Ways of describing difficulty believing something

The characters are confused and amazed by the disappearance of the train and find it hard to understand what has happened. This is expressed in a number of ways, some of which are shown in bold below.

4 Look at the vocabulary and definitions in the box below, and then use the words in bold to complete the sentences that follow.

> If something is **inexplicable**, it is impossible to explain.
> A **bewildering** situation is very confusing and difficult to understand.
> If you describe something as **lunacy**, you feel strongly that it is silly and even dangerous.
> **Consternation** is a shocked and worried feeling because something bad and unexpected happens.
> If people are **tearing their hair**, it is because they are very worried or annoyed about something and do not know what to do about it.
> If you are **disinclined** to do something, you are unwilling or reluctant.
> If something is **improbable**, it is not likely to happen or be true.
> If something is **feasible**, it is possible or likely to succeed.
> If you are **perplexed**, you are confused because you cannot understand something.

1 For some .... reason, she chose that moment to break the news.
2 Going outside in this storm would be ....
3 Her first day at work was extremely ....
4 She was as .... as the others as she stared at the map.
5 His comments caused .... among environmentalists.
6 There seems to be only one .... solution.
7 He was .... to believe her ridiculous story.
8 You can't be expected to believe me. I know it's a rather .... story.
9 The parents must be .... , not knowing where their children are.

Formal verbs

The story is written as an official report which uses very formal language – formal words, phrases and grammatical structures – to sound more serious and important. For example, it states that Monsieur Louis Caratal 'desired an interview with Mr James Bland', which could be expressed more simply: 'He wanted to speak with Mr James Bland'.

5 Read the sentences and match the formal verbs in bold with the more common, everyday verbs (a–j) below.

1 There are indications that the statement of this criminal is **corroborated** by the facts.
2 It may be as well to state the facts as far as we have been able to **ascertain** them.
3 The facts are **collated** from the records of the London and West Coast Railway Company.

4 A telegram was **dispatched** to each of the stations between St Helens and Manchester.

5 Both of them **manifested** extreme impatience to be off.

6 Mr. Horace Moore **alleged** that the sudden serious illness of his wife in London made it absolutely imperative that he should not lose an instant in starting upon the journey.

7 Nothing has **transpired** during these eight years which has shed the least light upon the extraordinary disappearance of the special train.

8 These names, which would shock all of Europe, shall not be **divulged.**

9 A month **elapsed**, during which both the police and the company carried out their inquiries without the slightest success.

10 Twelve of the branch lines have small-gauge lines. These can, of course, be **disregarded.**

a) find out	f) revealed
b) showed	g) came to be known
c) brought together	h) sent
d) ignored	i) supported
e) claimed	j) passed (time)

6 Replace a verb or phrase in these sentences with verbs in bold from 5 to make these sentences more formal. Make any necessary changes to the verbs and the sentences

a) The job involved the long, boring task of finding all the relevant papers and putting them together.

b) The defendant said that he was at home watching television at the time of the attack.

c) The clock on the operating theatre wall tells the anesthetist how much time has passed since the patient lost consciousness.

d) The police are trying to discover what really happened to Davis that night.

e) The judge asked the jury not to think about the comments of the last witness.

f) The newspaper journalists were reluctant to let the public know the name of the source in case it put his life at risk.

g) Over 30,000 leaflets had already been sent to local households before the error was noticed.

Main themes

Before you read the story, you may want to think about some of its main themes. The questions will help you think about the story as you are reading it for the first time. There is more discussion of the main themes in the *Literary analysis* section after the story.

Rational explanation

The story teller is very concerned with the facts of the case. He is precise in the smallest details, such as the fact that the special left the station 'at four thirty-one exactly by the station clock'. There is confidence that there is a rational explanation and that this explanation may be discovered providing that all the facts of the case are known. Emotions have no place in this story, then, and would only get in the way of the most important part of the story: the facts.

7 As you read the story, ask yourself:

a) Whose emotions does the story teller ignore? Whose does he discuss? Why?
b) Does the story teller ever let his emotions show at all? How do you think he feels about the missing train?
c) Is the final explanation for the mystery rational, in your opinion? If so, why? If not, why not?

Hindsight

The story is set eight years after the disappearance of the train. In a case as mysterious as this, it is impossible to know which details are important and which are irrelevant – unless you know what happened, of course. Hindsight is the opportunity to judge or understand past events using knowledge that you have gained since then. So we can say that the story teller includes many details that he might have ignored because in hindsight they are crucial to the solving of the mystery.

8 As you read the story, ask yourself:

a) With hindsight, do you think you could have predicted the answer to the mystery?
b) Do you think the investigators could have done anything to solve the mystery more quickly?

❓ The Lost Special

by Sir Arthur Conan Dyle

The confession of Herbert de Lernac, now lying under sentence of death at Marseilles, has thrown a light upon[2] one of the most inexplicable crimes of the century – an incident which is, I believe, absolutely unprecedented in the criminal **annals** of any country. Although there is a reluctance to discuss the matter in official circles, and little information has been given to the Press, there are still indications that the statement of this arch-criminal is corroborated by the facts, and that we have at last found a solution for a most astounding business. As the matter is eight years old, and as its importance was somewhat obscured by a political crisis which was engaging the public attention at the time, it may be as well to state the facts as far as we have been able to ascertain them. They are collated from the Liverpool papers of that date, from the proceedings at the **inquest** upon John Slater, the engine-driver, and from the records of the London and West Coast Railway Company, which have been courteously put at my disposal. Briefly, they are as follows:

On the 3rd of June, 1890, a gentleman, who gave his name as Monsieur Louis Caratal, desired an interview with Mr James Bland, the superintendent of the London and West Coast Central Station in Liverpool. He was a small man, middle-aged and dark, with a **stoop** which was so marked that it suggested some deformity of the spine. He was accompanied by a friend, a man of **imposing** physique, whose deferential manner and constant attention showed that his position was one of dependence. This friend or companion, whose name did not transpire, was certainly a foreigner, and probably from his swarthy[3] complexion, either a Spaniard or a South American.

---

2 *old-fashioned*: on
3 *mainly literary*: someone who is swarthy has dark skin

One peculiarity was observed in him. He carried in his left hand a small black, leather dispatch box[4], and it was noticed by a sharp-eyed clerk in the central office that this box was fastened to his wrist by a strap. No importance was attached to the fact at the time, but subsequent events endowed it with some significance. Monsieur Caratal was shown up to Mr Bland's office, while his companion remained outside.

Monsieur Caratal's business was quickly dispatched. He had arrived that afternoon from Central America. Affairs of the utmost importance demanded that he should be in Paris without the loss of an unnecessary hour. He had missed the London express. A special must be provided. Money was of no importance. Time was everything. If the company would speed him on his way, they might make their own terms.

Mr Bland struck the electric bell, summoned Mr Potter Hood, the traffic manager, and had the matter arranged in five minutes. The train would start in three-quarters of an hour. It would take that time to ensure that the line should be clear. The powerful engine called Rochdale (No. 247 on the company's register) was attached to two carriages, with a guard's van behind. The first carriage was solely for the purpose of decreasing the inconvenience arising from the oscillation[5]. The second was divided, as usual, into four compartments, a first-class, a first-class smoking, a second-class, and a second-class smoking. The first compartment, which was nearest to the engine, was the one allotted to the travellers. The other three were empty. The guard of the special train was James McPherson, who had been some years in the service of the company. The stoker, William Smith, was a new **hand**.

Monsieur Caratal, upon leaving the superintendent's office, rejoined his companion, and both of them manifested extreme impatience to be off. Having paid the money asked, which amounted to fifty pounds five shillings[6], at the usual special rate

4 *old-fashioned*: a case used for carrying important documents
5 *normally scientific*: a repeated movement from side to side at a steady speed; *here* the regular rocking motion of the train
6 *old-fashioned*: a small unit of money that was used in the UK until 1971

of five shillings a mile, they demanded to be shown the carriage, and at once took their seats in it, although they were assured that the better part of an hour must elapse before the line could be cleared. In the meantime a singular coincidence had occurred in the office which Monsieur Caratal had just quitted.

A request for a special is not a very uncommon circumstance in a rich commercial centre, but that two should be required upon the same afternoon was most unusual. It so happened, however, that Mr Bland had hardly dismissed the first traveller before a second entered with a similar request. This was a Mr Horace Moore, a gentlemanly man of military appearance, who alleged that the sudden serious illness of his wife in London made it absolutely imperative that he should not lose an instant in starting upon the journey. His distress and anxiety were so evident that Mr Bland did all that was possible to meet his wishes. A second special was out of the question, as the ordinary local service was already somewhat deranged[7] by the first. There was the alternative, however, that Mr Moore should share the expense of Monsieur Caratal's train, and should travel in the other empty first-class compartment, if Monsieur Caratal objected to having him in the one which he occupied. It was difficult to see any objection to such an arrangement, and yet Monsieur Caratal, upon the suggestion being made to him by Mr Potter Hood, absolutely refused to consider it for an instant. The train was his, he said, and he would insist upon the exclusive use of it. All argument failed to overcome his ungracious objections, and finally the plan had to be abandoned. Mr Horace Moore left the station in great distress, after learning that his only course was to take the ordinary slow train which leaves Liverpool at six o'clock. At four thirty-one exactly by the station clock the special train, containing the crippled[8] Monsieur Caratal and his gigantic companion, steamed out of the Liverpool station. The line was at that time clear, and there should have been no stoppage before Manchester.

7 *old-fashioned, uncommon*: disrupted, disturbed
8 *old-fashioned, offensive*: physically disabled, especially unable to walk

The trains of the London and West Coast Railway run over the lines of another company as far as this town, which should have been reached by the special rather before six o'clock. At a quarter after six considerable surprise and some consternation were caused amongst the officials at Liverpool by the receipt of a telegram from Manchester to say that it had not yet arrived. An inquiry directed to St Helens, which is a third of the way between the two cities, elicited the following reply –

'To James Bland, Superintendent, Central L. & W. C., Liverpool. – Special passed here at 4:52, well up to time. – Dowster, St Helens.'

This telegram was received at six-forty. At six-fifty a second message was received from Manchester –

'No sign of special as advised by you.'

And then ten minutes later a third, more bewildering –

'Presume some mistake as to proposed running of special. Local train from St Helens timed to follow it has just arrived and has seen nothing of it. Kindly wire advices[9]. – Manchester.'

The matter was assuming a most amazing aspect, although in some respects the last telegram was a relief to the authorities at Liverpool. If an accident had occurred to the special, it seemed hardly possible that the local train could have passed down the same line without observing it. And yet, what was the alternative? Where could the train be? Had it possibly been sidetracked[10] for some reason in order to allow the slower train to go past? Such an explanation was possible if some small repair had to be effected. A telegram was dispatched to each of the stations between St Helens and Manchester, and the superintendent and traffic manager waited in the utmost suspense at the instrument for the series of replies which would enable them to say for certain what had become of the missing train. The answers came back in the order of questions, which was the order of the stations beginning at the St Helens end –

'Special passed here five o'clock. – Collins Green.'

'Special passed here six past five. – Earlstown.'

9 *old-fashioned*: in modern usage, 'advice' is never countable
10 *technical*: if a train is sidetracked, it leaves the main line and takes a siding

'Special passed here 5:10. – Newton.'

'Special passed here 5:20. – Kenyon Junction.'

'No special train has passed here. – Barton Moss.'

The two officials stared at each other in amazement.

'This is unique in my thirty years of experience,' said Mr Bland.

'Absolutely **unprecedented** and inexplicable, sir. The special has gone wrong between Kenyon Junction and Barton Moss.'

'And yet there is no siding, so far as my memory serves me, between the two stations. The special must have run off the metals.'

'But how could the four-fifty parliamentary[11] pass over the same line without observing it?'

'There's no alternative, Mr Hood. It must be so. Possibly the local train may have observed something which may throw some light upon the matter. We will wire to Manchester for more information, and to Kenyon Junction with instructions that the line be examined instantly as far as Barton Moss.' The answer from Manchester came within a few minutes.

'No news of missing special. Driver and guard of slow train positive no accident between Kenyon Junction and Barton Moss. Line quite clear, and no sign of anything unusual. – Manchester.'

'That driver and guard will have to go,' said Mr Bland, **grimly**. 'There has been a wreck and they have missed it. The special has obviously run off the metals without disturbing the line – how it could have done so passes my comprehension – but so it must be, and we shall have a wire from Kenyon or Barton Moss presently to say that they have found her at the bottom of an embankment.'

But Mr Bland's prophecy was not destined to be fulfilled. Half an hour passed, and then there arrived the following message from the station-master of Kenyon Junction –

'There are no **traces** of the missing special. It is quite certain that she passed here, and that she did not arrive at Barton Moss.

11 *old-fashioned British*: a railway service provided by the government to ensure that poorer people could afford to travel

We have detached engine from goods train, and I have myself ridden down the line, but all is clear, and there is no sign of any accident.'

Mr Bland tore his hair in his perplexity.

'This is rank[12] lunacy, Hood!' he cried. 'Does a train vanish into thin air in England in broad daylight? The thing is **preposterous**. An engine, a tender, two carriages, a van, five human beings – and all lost on a straight line of railway! Unless we get something positive within the next hour I'll take Inspector Collins, and go down myself.'

And then at last something positive did occur. It took the shape of another telegram from Kenyon Junction.

'Regret to report that the dead body of John Slater, driver of the special train, has just been found among the gorse bushes at a point two and a quarter miles from the Junction. Had fallen from his engine, pitched down the embankment, and rolled among the bushes. Injuries to his head, from the fall, appear to be cause of death. Ground has now been carefully examined, and there is no trace of the missing train.'

The country was, as has already been stated, **in the throes** of a political crisis, and the attention of the public was further distracted by the important and sensational developments in Paris, where a huge scandal threatened to destroy the Government and to wreck the reputations of many of the leading men in France. The papers were full of these events, and the singular disappearance of the special train attracted less attention than would have been the case in more peaceful times. The **grotesque** nature of the event helped to detract from its importance, for the papers were disinclined to believe the facts as reported to them. More than one of the London journals treated the matter as an ingenious **hoax**, until the **coroner**'s inquest upon the unfortunate driver (an inquest which elicited nothing of importance) convinced them of the tragedy of the incident.

Mr Bland, accompanied by Inspector Collins, the senior detective officer in the service of the company, went down to

12 *uncommon*: complete, used for emphasizing how bad or obvious something is

Kenyon Junction the same evening, and their research lasted throughout the following day, but was attended[13] with purely negative results. Not only was no trace found of the missing train, but no conjecture[14] could be put forward which could possibly explain the facts. At the same time, Inspector Collins's official report (which lies before[15] me as I write) served to show that the possibilities were more numerous than might have been expected.

'In the stretch of railway between these two points,' said he, 'the country is dotted with ironworks and collieries. Of these, some are being worked and some have been abandoned. There are no fewer than twelve which have small-gauge lines which run trolly-cars down to the main line. These can, of course, be disregarded. Besides these, however, there are seven which have, or have had, proper lines running down and connecting with points to the main line, so as to convey their produce from the mouth of the mine to the great centres of distribution. In every case these lines are only a few miles in length. Out of the seven, four belong to collieries which are worked out[16], or at least to **shafts** which are no longer used. These are the Redgauntlet, Hero, Slough of Despond, and Heartsease mines, the latter having ten years ago been one of the principal mines in Lancashire. These four side lines may be eliminated from our inquiry, for, to prevent possible accidents, the rails nearest to the main line have been taken up, and there is no longer any connection. There remain three other side lines leading –

(a) To the Carnstock Iron Works;
(b) To the Big Ben Colliery;
(c) To the Perseverance Colliery.

'Of these the Big Ben line is not more than a quarter of a mile long, and ends at a dead wall of coal waiting removal from the mouth of the mine. Nothing had been seen or heard there of any special. The Carnstock Iron Works line was blocked all day upon

13 *old-fashioned, formal, unusual*: to accompany, or have something as a result
14 *formal*: a theory or guess based on information that is not complete
15 *literary*: in front of
16 *technical*: a mine which has been worked out has had all the coal removed from it

the 3rd of June by sixteen truckloads of hematite[17]. It is a single line, and nothing could have passed. As to the Perseverance line, it is a large double line, which does a considerable traffic, for the output of the mine is very large. On the 3rd of June this traffic proceeded as usual; hundreds of men including a gang of railway platelayers were working along the two miles and a quarter which constitute the total length of the line, and it is inconceivable that an unexpected train could have come down there without attracting universal attention. It may be remarked in conclusion that this branch line is nearer to St Helens than the point at which the engine-driver was discovered, so that we have every reason to believe that the train was past that point before misfortune overtook her.

'As to John Slater, there is no clue to be gathered from his appearance or injuries. We can only say that, so far as we can see, he met his end by falling off his engine, though why he fell, or what became of the engine after his fall, is a question upon which I do not feel qualified to offer an opinion.' In conclusion, the inspector offered his resignation to the Board[18], being much nettled[19] by an accusation of incompetence in the London papers.

A month elapsed, during which both the police and the company prosecuted their inquiries without the slightest success. A reward was offered and a pardon promised in case of crime, but they were both unclaimed. Every day the public opened their papers with the conviction that so grotesque a mystery would at last be solved, but week after week passed by, and a solution remained as far off as ever. In broad daylight, upon a June afternoon in the most thickly inhabited portion of England, a train with its occupants had disappeared as completely as if some master of **subtle** chemistry had volatilized it into gas. Indeed, among the various conjectures which were put forward in the public Press, there were some which seriously

17 (US spelling, UK spelling: haematite) a red rock from which iron is obtained
18 a group of people who have the responsibility of managing important business or government activities, in this case, the railway company
19 informal: annoyed

asserted that supernatural, or, at least, preternatural[20], agencies had been at work, and that the deformed Monsieur Caratal was probably a person who was better known under a less polite name. Others fixed upon his swarthy companion as being the author of the **mischief**, but what it was exactly which he had done could never be clearly formulated in words.

Amongst the many suggestions put forward by various newspapers or private individuals, there were one or two which were feasible enough to attract the attention of the public. One which appeared in The Times, over the signature of an amateur reasoner of some celebrity at that date, attempted to deal with the matter in a critical and semi-scientific manner. An extract must suffice, although the curious can see the whole letter in the issue of the 3rd of July.

'It is one of the elementary principles of practical reasoning,' he remarked, 'that when the impossible has been eliminated the residuum[21], HOWEVER IMPROBABLE, must contain the truth. It is certain that the train left Kenyon Junction. It is certain that it did not reach Barton Moss. It is in the highest degree unlikely, but still possible, that it may have taken one of the seven available side lines. It is obviously impossible for a train to run where there are no rails, and, therefore, we may reduce our improbables to the three open lines, namely the Carnstock Iron Works, the Big Ben, and the Perseverance. Is there a secret society of colliers[22], an English Camorra[23], which is capable of destroying both train and passengers? It is improbable, but it is not impossible. I confess that I am unable to suggest any other solution. I should certainly advise the company to direct all their energies towards the observation of those three lines, and of the workmen at the end of them. A careful supervision of the **pawnbrokers**' shops of the district might possibly bring some suggestive facts to light.'

20 *formal*: extremely strange and often involving abilities or qualities that people do
   not normally have
21 *scientific*: something remaining after removal of a part
22 *old-fashioned*: coal miners
23 a criminal organization which has its roots in Naples in the South of Italy

The suggestion coming from a recognized authority upon such matters created considerable interest, and a fierce opposition from those who considered such a statement to be a preposterous **libel** upon an honest and deserving set of men. The only answer to this criticism was a challenge to the objectors to lay any more feasible explanations before the public. In reply to this two others were forthcoming[24] (Times, July 7th and 9th). The first suggested that the train might have run off the metals and be lying submerged in the Lancashire and Staffordshire Canal, which runs parallel to the railway for some hundred of yards. This suggestion was thrown out of court by the published depth of the canal, which was entirely insufficient to conceal so large an object. The second correspondent wrote calling attention to the bag which appeared to be the sole luggage which the travellers had brought with them, and suggesting that some novel explosive of immense and pulverizing[25] power might have been concealed in it. The obvious absurdity, however, of supposing that the whole train might be blown to dust while the metals remained uninjured reduced any such explanation to a **farce**. The investigation had drifted into this hopeless position when a new and most unexpected incident occurred.

This was nothing less than the receipt by Mrs McPherson of a letter from her husband, James McPherson, who had been the guard on the missing train. The letter, which was dated July 5th, 1890, was posted from New York and came to hand upon July 14th. Some doubts were expressed as to its genuine character but Mrs McPherson was positive as to the writing, and the fact that it contained a remittance[26] of a hundred dollars in five-dollar notes was enough in itself to discount the idea of a hoax. No address was given in the letter, which ran in this way:

MY DEAR WIFE, –

'I have been thinking a great deal, and I find it very hard to give you up. The same with Lizzie. I try to fight against it, but it will always come back to me. I send you some money which will

24 *formal*: provided or available when needed or asked for
25 *technical*: to crush something into very small pieces
26 *formal*: a payment for goods or services that you send by post

change into twenty English pounds. This should be enough to bring both Lizzie and you across the Atlantic, and you will find the Hamburg boats which stop at Southampton very good boats, and cheaper than Liverpool. If you could come here and stop at the Johnston House I would try and send you word how to meet, but things are very difficult with me at present, and I am not very happy, finding it hard to give you both up. So no more at present, from your loving husband,

James McPherson.'

For a time it was confidently anticipated that this letter would lead to the clearing up of the whole matter, the more so as it was ascertained that a passenger who **bore a close resemblance** to the missing guard had travelled from Southampton under the name of Summers in the Hamburg and New York liner Vistula, which started upon the 7th of June. Mrs McPherson and her sister Lizzie Dolton went across to New York as directed and stayed for three weeks at the Johnston House, without hearing anything from the missing man. It is probable that some injudicious[27] comments in the Press may have warned him that the police were using them as a **bait**. However this may be, it is certain that he neither wrote nor came, and the women were eventually compelled to return to Liverpool.

And so the matter stood, and has continued to stand up to the present year of 1898. Incredible as it may seem, nothing has transpired during these eight years which has shed the least light upon the extraordinary disappearance of the special train which contained Monsieur Caratal and his companion. Careful inquiries into the antecedents[28] of the two travellers have only established the fact that Monsieur Caratal was well known as a financier and political agent in Central America, and that during his voyage to Europe he had betrayed extraordinary anxiety to reach Paris. His companion, whose name was entered upon the passenger lists as Eduardo Gomez, was a man whose record was a violent one, and whose reputation was that of a bravo[29]

27 *formal*: not showing careful thought or good judgment
28 *very formal*: in this context it refers to the history and background of the two men
29 *old-fashioned*: a thug or hired assassin

and a bully. There was evidence to show, however, that he was honestly devoted to the interests of Monsieur Caratal, and that the latter, being a man of **puny** physique, employed the other as a guard and protector. It may be added that no information came from Paris as to what the objects[30] of Monsieur Caratal's hurried journey may have been. This comprises all the facts of the case up to the publication in the Marseilles papers of the recent confession of Herbert de Lernac, now under sentence of death for the murder of a merchant named Bonvalot. This statement may be literally translated as follows:

'It is not out of mere pride or **boasting** that I give this information, for, if that were my object, I could tell a dozen actions of mine which are quite as splendid; but I do it in order that certain gentlemen in Paris may understand that I, who am able here to tell about the fate of Monsieur Caratal, can also tell in whose interest and at whose request the **deed** was done, unless the **reprieve** which I am awaiting comes to me very quickly. Take warning, messieurs[31], before it is too late! You know Herbert de Lernac, and you are aware that his deeds are as ready as his words. Hasten[32] then, or you are lost!

'At present I shall mention no names – if you only heard the names, what would you not think! – but I shall merely tell you how cleverly I did it. I was true to my employers then, and no doubt they will be true to me now. I hope so, and until I am convinced that they have betrayed me, these names, which would convulse[33] Europe, shall not be divulged. But on that day . . . well, I say no more!

'In a word, then, there was a famous trial in Paris, in the year 1890, in connection with a monstrous scandal in politics and finance. How monstrous that scandal was can never be known save by such confidential agents as myself. The honour and careers of many of the chief men in France were **at stake**. You have seen a group of ninepins[34] standing, all so rigid, and

---

30 *old-fashioned*: something that you plan to achieve
31 *French*: gentlemen (the singular is *monsieur*)
32 *literary*: hurry
33 *journalistic*: to cause major problems or serious harm to someone or something
34 *old-fashioned*: a wooden object shaped like a bottle, similar to pins used in modern-day ten-pin bowling

prim, and unbending. Then there comes the ball from far away and pop, pop, pop – there are your ninepins on the floor. Well, imagine some of the greatest men in France as these ninepins and then this Monsieur Caratal was the ball which could be seen coming from far away. If he arrived, then it was pop, pop, pop for all of them. It was determined that he should not arrive.

'I do not accuse them all of being conscious of what was to happen. There were, as I have said, great financial as well as political interests at stake, and a syndicate[35] was formed to manage the business. Some subscribed to the syndicate who hardly understood what were its objects. But others understood very well, and they can rely upon it that I have not forgotten their names. They had **ample** warning that Monsieur Caratal was coming long before he left South America, and they knew that the evidence which he held would certainly mean ruin to all of them. The syndicate had the command of an unlimited amount of money – absolutely unlimited, you understand. They looked round for an agent who was capable of **wielding** this gigantic power. The man chosen must be inventive, resolute, adaptive – a man in a million. They chose Herbert de Lernac, and I admit that they were right.

'My duties were to choose my subordinates[36], to use freely the power which money gives, and to make certain that Monsieur Caratal should never arrive in Paris. With characteristic energy I set about my commission within an hour of receiving my instructions, and the steps which I took were the very best for the purpose which could possibly be devised.

'A man whom I could trust was dispatched instantly to South America to travel home with Monsieur Caratal. Had he arrived in time the ship would never have reached Liverpool; but alas![37] it had already started before my agent could reach it. I fitted out a small armed brig[38] to intercept it, but again I was unfortunate. Like all great organizers I was, however, prepared for failure,

35 a group of people or organizations that work together to achieve a particular aim
36 *formal*: someone who has less power or authority than someone else
37 *old-fashioned*: an exclamation used when you are sad about something and you wish it had not happened
38 a ship with two masts and square sails

and had a series of alternatives prepared, one or the other of which must succeed. You must not underrate the difficulties of my **undertaking**, or imagine that a mere commonplace assassination would meet the case. We must destroy not only Monsieur Caratal, but Monsieur Caratal's documents, and Monsieur Caratal's companions also, if we had reason to believe that he had communicated his secrets to them. And you must remember that they were on the alert, and keenly suspicious of any such attempt. It was a task which was in every way worthy of me, for I am always most masterful where another would be **appalled**.

'I was all ready for Monsieur Caratal's reception[39] in Liverpool, and I was the more eager because I had reason to believe that he had made arrangements by which he would have a considerable guard from the moment that he arrived in London. Anything which was to be done must be done between the moment of his setting foot upon the Liverpool **quay** and that of his arrival at the London and West Coast terminus in London. We prepared six plans, each more elaborate than the last; which plan would be used would depend upon his own movements. Do what he would, we were ready for him. If he had stayed in Liverpool, we were ready. If he took an ordinary train, an express, or a special, all was ready. Everything had been foreseen and provided for. 'You may imagine that I could not do all this myself. What could I know of the English railway lines? But money can procure willing agents all the world over, and I soon had one of the **acutest** brains in England to assist me. I will mention no names, but it would be unjust to claim all the credit for myself. My English **ally** was worthy of such an alliance. He knew the London and West Coast line thoroughly, and he had the command of a band of workers who were trustworthy and intelligent. The idea was his, and my own judgement was only required in the details. We bought over[40] several officials, amongst whom the most important was James McPherson, whom

39 *formal*: arrival
40 *unusual*: if you buy someone over, you bribe them, or pay them in return for a favour

we had ascertained to be the guard most likely to be employed upon a special train. Smith, the stoker, was also in our employ. John Slater, the engine-driver, had been approached, but had been found to be **obstinate** and dangerous, so we desisted[41]. We had no certainty that Monsieur Caratal would take a special, but we thought it very probable, for it was of the utmost importance to him that he should reach Paris without delay. It was for this contingency[42], therefore, that we made special preparations – preparations which were complete down to the last detail long before his steamer had sighted the shores of England. You will be amused to learn that there was one of my agents in the pilot-boat which brought that steamer to its **moorings**.

'The moment that Caratal arrived in Liverpool we knew that he suspected danger and was on his guard. He had brought with him as an escort a dangerous fellow, named Gomez, a man who carried weapons, and was prepared to use them. This fellow carried Caratal's confidential papers for him, and was ready to protect either them or his master. The probability was that Caratal had taken him into his counsels[43], and that to remove Caratal without removing Gomez would be a mere waste of energy. It was necessary that they should be involved in a common fate, and our plans to that end were much facilitated by their request for a special train. On that special train you will understand that two out of the three servants of the company were really in our employ, at a price which would make them independent for a lifetime. I do not go so far as to say that the English are more honest than any other nation, but I have found them more expensive to buy.

'I have already spoken of my English agent – who is a man with a considerable future before him, unless some complaint of the throat carries him off before his time. He had charge of all arrangements at Liverpool, whilst I was stationed at the inn at Kenyon, where I awaited a cipher[44] signal to act. When the

41 *formal*: to stop doing something
42 *formal*: a situation that might happen in the future
43 *formal, legal*: if you take someone into your counsels, you tell them something secret or private
44 *technical*: a secret system of writing, used for sending messages

special was arranged for, my agent instantly telegraphed to me and warned me how soon I should have everything ready. He himself, under the name of Horace Moore, applied immediately for a special also, in the hope that he would be sent down with Monsieur Caratal, which might under certain circumstances have been helpful to us. If, for example, our great coup[45] had failed, it would then have become the duty of my agent to have shot them both and destroyed their papers. Caratal was on his guard, however, and refused to admit any other traveller. My agent then left the station, returned by another entrance, entered the guard's van on the side farthest from the platform, and travelled down with McPherson the guard.

'In the meantime you will be interested to know what my movements were. Everything had been prepared for days before, and only the finishing touches were needed. The side line which we had chosen had once joined the main line, but it had been disconnected. We had only to replace a few rails to connect it once more. These rails had been laid down as far as could be done without danger of attracting attention, and now it was merely a case of completing a juncture with the line, and arranging the points as they had been before. The sleepers had never been removed, and the rails, fish-plates and rivets[46] were all ready, for we had taken them from a siding on the abandoned portion of the line. With my small but competent band of workers, we had everything ready long before the special arrived. When it did arrive, it ran off upon the small side line so easily that the **jolting** of the points appears to have been entirely unnoticed by the two travellers.

'Our plan had been that Smith, the stoker, should chloroform[47] John Slater, the driver, so that he should vanish with the others. In this respect, and in this respect only, our plans miscarried[48] – I except the criminal folly[49] of McPherson in writing home to

45 an impressive and surprising success
46 *technical*: various parts fixing the rails of a railway solidly to the ground
47 to make someone breathe *chloroform* – a clear liquid with a strong smell that makes you become unconscious if you breathe it
48 *mainly literary*: if a plan or activity miscarries, it fails or goes wrong
49 *formal*: a way of behaving that is stupid and careless, and likely to have bad results

his wife. Our stoker did his business so clumsily that Slater in his struggles fell off the engine, and though fortune was with us so far that he broke his neck in the fall, still he remained as a blot[50] upon that which would otherwise have been one of those complete masterpieces which are only to be contemplated in silent admiration. The criminal expert will find in John Slater the one **flaw** in all our admirable combinations. A man who has had as many triumphs as I can afford to be frank, and I therefore lay my finger upon John Slater, and I proclaim him to be a flaw.

'But now I have got our special train upon the small line two kilometres, or rather more than one mile, in length, which leads, or rather used to lead, to the abandoned Heartsease mine, once one of the largest coal mines in England. You will ask how it is that no one saw the train upon this unused line. I answer that along its entire length it runs through a deep cutting, and that, unless someone had been on the edge of that cutting, he could not have seen it. There WAS someone on the edge of that cutting. I was there. And now I will tell you what I saw.

'My assistant had remained at the points in order that he might superintend the switching off of the train. He had four armed men with him, so that if the train ran off the line – we thought it probable, because the points were very rusty – we might still have resources to fall back upon. Having once seen it safely on the side line, he handed over the responsibility to me. I was waiting at a point which overlooks the mouth of the mine, and I was also armed, as were my two companions. Come what might[51], you see, I was always ready.

'The moment that the train was fairly on the side line, Smith, the stoker, slowed-down the engine, and then, having turned it on to the fullest speed again, he and McPherson, with my English lieutenant, sprang off before it was too late. It may be that it was this slowing-down which first attracted the attention of the travellers, but the train was running at full speed again before their heads appeared at the open window. It makes me

50 *literary*: something that spoils someone's reputation, or spoils the appearance of something
51 *literary, formal*: 'come what might', or more often, 'come what may' means despite anything that may happen

smile to think how bewildered they must have been. Picture to yourself your own feelings if, on looking out of your luxurious carriage, you suddenly perceived that the lines upon which you ran were rusted and corroded, red and yellow with disuse and decay! What a catch must have come in their breath as in a second it flashed upon[52] them that it was not Manchester but Death which was waiting for them at the end of that sinister line. But the train was running with frantic speed, rolling and rocking over the rotten line, while the wheels made a frightful screaming sound upon the rusted surface. I was close to them, and could see their faces. Caratal was praying, I think – there was something like a rosary[53] dangling out of his hand. The other roared like a bull who smells the blood of the **slaughter house**. He saw us standing on the bank, and he **beckoned** to us like a madman. Then he tore at his wrist and threw his dispatch-box out of the window in our direction. Of course, his meaning was obvious. Here was the evidence, and they would promise to be silent if their lives were spared. It would have been very agreeable if we could have done so, but business is business. Besides, the train was now as much beyond our controls as theirs.

'He ceased howling when the train rattled round the curve and they saw the black mouth of the mine yawning[54] before them. We had removed the boards which had covered it, and we had cleared the square entrance. The rails had formerly run very close to the shaft for the convenience of loading the coal, and we had only to add two or three lengths of rail in order to lead to the very brink[55] of the shaft. In fact, as the lengths would not quite fit, our line projected about three feet over the edge. We saw the two heads at the window: Caratal below, Gomez above; but they had both been struck silent by what they saw. And yet they could not withdraw their heads. The sight seemed to have paralysed them.

52 *literary*: if something flashes upon you, you suddenly realize or remember something
53 a set of small beads used by Roman Catholics for praying
54 to open your mouth to take a big breath, usually because you are tired or bored. Here the writer uses *yawn* as a metaphor to say that the opening of the mine is like an open mouth.
55 *literary*: the top of a very steep cliff

'I had wondered how the train running at a great speed would take the pit into which I had guided it, and I was much interested in watching it. One of my colleagues thought that it would actually jump it, and indeed it was not very far from doing so. Fortunately, however, it fell short, and the buffers[56] of the engine struck the other lip of the shaft with a tremendous crash. The funnel[57] flew off into the air. The tender, carriages, and van were all smashed up into one jumble, which, with the remains of the engine, choked for a minute or so the mouth of the pit. Then something gave way in the middle, and the whole mass of green iron, smoking coals, brass fittings, wheels, wood-work, and cushions all crumbled together and crashed down into the mine. We heard the rattle, rattle, rattle, as the debris struck against the walls, and then, quite a long time afterwards, there came a deep roar as the remains of the train struck the bottom. The boiler may have burst, for a sharp crash came after the roar, and then a dense cloud of steam and smoke swirled up out of the black depths, falling in a spray as thick as rain all round us. Then the vapour shredded off into thin wisps, which floated away in the summer sunshine, and all was quiet again in the Heartsease mine.

'And now, having carried out our plans so successfully, it only remained to leave no trace behind us. Our little band of workers at the other end had already ripped up the rails and disconnected the side line, replacing everything as it had been before. We were equally busy at the mine. The funnel and other fragments were thrown in, the shaft was planked over as it used to be, and the lines which led to it were torn up and taken away. Then, without flurry, but without delay, we all made our way out of the country, most of us to Paris, my English colleague to Manchester, and McPherson to Southampton, whence he emigrated to America. Let the English papers of that date tell how thoroughly we had done our work, and how completely we had thrown the cleverest of their detectives off our track.

56 *British*: one of two metal springs at the front and back of a train and at the end of a railway line that helps to protect the train if it crashes
57 the chimney of a steam engine

'You will remember that Gomez threw his bag of papers out of the window, and I need not say that I secured that bag and brought them to my employers. It may interest my employers now, however, to learn that out of that bag I took one or two little papers as a souvenir of the occasion. I have no wish to publish these papers; but, still, it is every man for himself in this world, and what else can I do if my friends will not come to my aid when I want them? Messieurs, you may believe that Herbert de Lernac is quite as **formidable** when he is against you as when he is with you, and that he is not a man to go to the guillotine[58] until he has seen that every one of you is en route for New Caledonia[59]. For your own sake, if not for mine, make haste, Monsieur de -- , and General -- , and Baron --(you can fill up the blanks for yourselves as you read this). I promise you that in the next edition there will be no blanks to fill.

'P.S. – As I look over my statement there is only one omission which I can see. It concerns the unfortunate man McPherson, who was foolish enough to write to his wife and to make an appointment with her in New York. It can be imagined that when interests like ours were at stake, we could not leave them to the chance of whether a man in that class of life would or would not give away his secrets to a woman. Having once broken his **oath** by writing to his wife, we could not trust him any more. We took steps therefore to insure that he should not see his wife. I have sometimes thought that it would be a kindness to write to her and to assure her that there is no impediment[60] to her marrying again.'

---

58 a machine used in the past for cutting off someone's head, made famous during the French Revolution
59 a group of islands in the Pacific Ocean, a former colony of France. There was a prison where French criminals were sent during the nineteenth century
60 *formal*: something that makes it more difficult for someone to do something or more difficult for something to happen

Post-reading exercises

Understanding the story

Use these questions to help you check that you have understood the story.

The account of the disappearance

1 Why is the story being told now, so long after the event?
2 Why do you think there is 'a reluctance to discuss the matter in official circles'?
3 Where do the details of the story come from, according to the story teller?
4 What does Caratal's decision to pay for a special train indicate?
5 How many people were on the train in total? Who were they?
6 Why do you think Caratal refuses to let Horace Moore share the special?
7 Put the stations in order, from nearest to Liverpool to nearest to Manchester: Barton Moss, Collins Green, Earlstown, Kenyon Junction, Newton, St Helens. Where does the train disappear?

Reports and theories

8 Why does the news of the missing train receive so little attention?
9 In total, how many side lines are there between Kenyon Junction and Barton Moss? Why are twelve of them not investigated? What about the others? Why do the authorities assume that these others were not used to hide the train?
10 Why is the solution suggested by the 'amateur reasoner' so unpopular with many people?
11 What is the significance of the letter from James McPherson?

Herbert de Lernac's statement

12 What was de Lernac's objective in making the train 'disappear'?
13 Why does he confess the crime now, eight years later?
14 Why was it so important that he fulfil his mission before Caratal arrived in London?
15 Why does he say: 'there was one of my agents in the pilot-boat which brought that steamer to its moorings'?
16 What do you think he means when he says of his English agent that he is 'a man with a considerable future before him, unless some complaint of the throat carries him off before his time'?
17 What, according to de Lernac, was the only mistake that was made in the plan?

18 What steps did the criminals take to hide their crime?
19 Why does he mention the 'one or two little papers' that he took 'as a souvenir'?
20 What does he mean when talking about McPherson's wife that 'there is no impediment to her marrying again'?

Language study

Grammar

Speculating about the past – past modal verbs

Throughout the story people try to make sense of the mystery. They 'speculate', that is they consider or discuss it without knowing all the facts. They suggest several theories to explain the disappearance. Some sound more certain than others.

The modal verbs **must**, **might**, **may**, **could**, **might not**, **may not**, **couldn't**, and **can't** can be used with the perfect infinitive **have + past participle** (*been, done, etc*) to speculate about the past. Verb phrases and adverbs can also be used to speculate about the past.

1 **Look at the following sentences from the story and underline the modal verbs and other phrases that express speculation. The first have been done for you.**

1 If an accident had occurred to the special, <u>it seemed hardly possible that</u> the local train <u>could have passed</u> down the same line without observing it. And yet, what was the alternative?

2 There's no alternative, Mr Hood. It must be so. Possibly the local train may have observed something which may throw some light upon the matter.

3 The special has obviously run off the metals without disturbing the line – how it could have done so passes my comprehension – but so it must be.

4 It is a single line, and nothing could have passed.

5 … it is inconceivable that an unexpected train could have come down there without attracting universal attention.

6 It is in the highest degree unlikely, but still possible, that it may have taken one of the seven available side lines.

2 **Answer the questions.**

1 Which modals express that the speaker is sure something happened? What other phrases express this?

2 Which modals express that the speaker believes something possibly happened? What other phrases express this?

3 Which modals express that the speaker is sure something didn't happen? What other phrases express this?

Could, *may* and *might* all have a similar meaning when they are used to speculate about the past, but they are not identical. Firstly, when used in the negative, *couldn't have* means *it is not possible*, whereas *may not have* and *might not have* mean *it is possible that it wasn't*. Compare these two sentences:

*The train **couldn't have been blown up** or else the track would have been damaged.*

*The train **might not have been destroyed** on the track. It may have come off the line first.*

Remember, too, that we only use *can* in the negative when speculating about the past, with the same meaning as *could*.

In affirmative sentences, *might* often implies *there is a small chance*, whereas *may* and *could* often imply *there is a good chance*. Context and intonation help to determine the exact meaning.

3 Choose the correct verb to complete the sentences.

1 The train driver **might/can't/mustn't** have known about the plan if they had asked him to join the team.

2 Caratal **might/may/must** have been very scared if he knew that they were planning to kill him.

3 Before the train started, the superintendent **must/can/can't** have sent telegrams to all the stations to warn them that a special was on its way.

4 There was always a risk that someone **can/may/must** have seen something strange if they were near the Heartsease mine.

5 If the driver hadn't died when he fell from the train, he **must/might/can't** have been able to tell the police what really happened.

6 The amateur reasoner **couldn't/mustn't/may not** have been Sherlock Holmes because he always solved his mysteries!

4 Use a modal verb to rewrite the sentences so that the meaning stays the same.

e.g. It is inconceivable that the climbers survived the whole winter in the mountains.

The climbers can't/couldn't have survived the whole winter ...

1 They died weeks ago; there's no question otherwise.

2 It is unlikely, but still possible, that the rescue team have found the bodies and are on their way back.
3 They obviously had an accident, which is why they didn't make it back to base camp.
4 It seems impossible to imagine that they found any food at that altitude.
5 With the GPS technology that they had, is it possible that they got lost?

Subjunctive use of *should*

The world of *The Lost Special* is a busy place full of important people with big responsibilities and little time. Two common structures which express an idea of urgency and importance are: verb + *that* + *should*, and verb + *that* + subjunctive. They are very formal structures:

*Affairs of the utmost importance **demanded that** he **should be** in Paris.*

*My duties were … to **make certain that** Monsieur Caratal **should** never arrive in Paris.*

These sentences can also be expressed using the subjunctive:

*Affairs of the utmost importance **demanded that** he **be** in Paris.*

*My duties were … to **make certain that** Monsieur Caratal never **arrive** in Paris.*

The verb in the subjunctive looks the same as the infinitive and so it is only noticeable in certain forms:

You try to solve the case. (not subjunctive)

*It is important that you **try** to solve the case.* (subjunctive)

She tries to solve the case. (not subjunctive)

*It is important that she **try** to solve the case.* (subjunctive)

Negative sentences take *not*:

*… the sudden serious illness of his wife in London **made it absolutely imperative** that he (**should**) **not lose** an instant in starting upon the journey.*

5 **Complete the second sentence so that it means the same as the first. Use either *should* or the subjunctive.**

e.g. Holmes asked Watson to accompany him to the house.
Holmes requested …
Holmes requested (that) Watson (should) accompany him to the house.

1 Michael wants you to join the committee.
  Michael recommends …

2 Does she have to be there?
  Is it essential …?

3 The company doesn't want employees to accept personal phone
  calls during business hours.
  The company asks …

4 We can't stress enough the importance of taking plenty of water
  with you on this journey.
  It is highly recommended …

5 I couldn't let Harold's partner read the letter before he did.
  It was of utmost importance that Harold …

**6 Many verbs that take the subjunctive are reporting verbs, such
  as *recommend, suggest* and *ask*. Report these sentences using the
  should or subjunctive structure. Choose an appropriate reporting
  verb: *recommend,* suggest, *request,* or *insist*.**

e.g. Teacher to students: 'You must be on time for class.'
The teacher insisted that students (should) be on time.

1 Doctor to patient: 'I really think it would be a good idea to see a
  specialist about the problem.'
2 Manager to employee: 'If I were you, I wouldn't take the job without
  renegotiating the salary.'
3 Bank Manager to Mrs Graham (customer): 'Can I ask you to sign
  this letter, Mrs Graham?'
4 Skin specialist to client: 'Always wear a sun cream SPF15 or higher.'

Vocabulary

Metaphorical language – Understanding is seeing

Images of light and seeing are often used as metaphors for
understanding and knowledge. Think of the image of a light bulb
shining over someone's head to signify a 'bright' idea. The literal
meaning of 'bright' is 'full of strong shining light'; the metaphorical

meaning is 'intelligent'. Visibility, or the lack of it, is used in *The Lost Special* as a metaphor to describe the confusion surrounding the crime.

7 Look at the examples from the story (a–d) and match them to their definitions (1–4).

a **to obscure**

Its importance was somewhat obscured by a political crisis which was engaging the public attention at the time.

b **throw/shed/cast light on something**

Possibly the local train may have observed something which may throw some light upon the matter.

Nothing has transpired during these eight years which has shed the least light upon the extraordinary disappearance of the special train.

c **bring something to light**

A careful supervision of the pawnbrokers' shops might bring some facts to light.

d **flash/dawn upon/on someone**

In a second it flashed upon them that it was not Manchester but Death which was waiting for them at the end of that sinister line.

1 to provide new information that helps you understand something
2 to realize something for the first time
3 to find new facts or evidence
4 to make something difficult to understand

8 Cross out the words which do not collocate.

1 to throw/shed/bring light on a matter/facts/mystery
2 to bring facts/the mystery/new evidence to light
3 to obscure the facts/matter/mystery
4 to flash/dawn/light on someone that …

9 Use idioms from exercise 7 to complete the sentences.

1 New evidence in this case has recently ....
2 I had hoped that he would be able to .... on the problem.
3 This accident should not .... the fact that train travel is extremely safe.
4 It suddenly .... Tom that his wife was not coming back.

Literary analysis

Plot

1 Make a list of the main events leading up to the disappearance of the train and the main events that happen after it. Are they described in the order in which they happen?

2 The story gives a lot of detail about a number of things that are not central to the plot. Why does the writer talk so much about:
   a) the second special?
   b) the employees on the train?
   c) the train itself, its engine, carriages and so on?
   d) the side lines, collieries and ironworks near the main line?

3 On the other hand, the writer doesn't give much detail about 'the important and sensational developments in Paris', even though they are mentioned several times throughout the story. Why not?

4 Did you predict the solution to the mystery at all? Could you? Are there any clues that might help you to arrive at a correct prediction?

5 What kind of information might Caratal have known that would create such a powerful motive to have him killed?

6 What do you think happens to de Lernac after the end of the story?

7 What do you think the British authorities should do now that they have read de Lernac's confession?

8 How believable is the story, in your opinion?

Character

9 Who are the main characters in the story?

10 What do we know about Louis Caratal? What does he look like? What about his personality? What information can you deduce from his actions?

11 Do you feel sorry for Caratal and his companion, Eduardo Gomez? Why/Why not? Would you feel differently if you knew more about their mission to Paris?

12 We are not given much information about the other characters, such as James Bland, the station superintendent, and James McPherson, the guard working on the special who flees to America. In keeping with the style of an official report, this information is irrelevant. However, the writer conveys something about their personalities in the way they act and speak. What kind of person is James Bland, the station superintendent? What about James McPherson, the special guard who escapes to America?

13 What is your impression of Herbert de Lernac from the way he narrates his side of the story? What is his opinion about his own abilities? What about his interest in the final moments of the train and the deaths of Caratal and Gomez? What does that tell you about him?

Narration

14 Why do you think the story teller is telling the story? What might his or her job be? Who is he or she telling it to?

15 Would you say that the main narrator is a character in the story? What impression, if any, do you have of him/her?

16 Put the different texts in the order in which they are used to tell the story:
   a) Herbert de Lernac's statement to the French police (translated)
   b) Inspector Collins's report
   c) letter from James McPherson to his wife
   d) letter from *The Times*, dated 3rd July
   e) letters from *The Times*, dated 7th and 9th July
   f) telegrams from the main line station masters

17 What other sources of information does the story teller claim to have used to complete this report?

18 Read this extract and answer the questions.

One [suggestion] which appeared in The Times, over the signature of an amateur reasoner of some celebrity at that date, attempted to deal with the matter in a critical and semi-scientific manner. An extract must suffice, although the curious can see the whole letter in the issue of the 3rd of July.

Why does the writer claim that this is just an extract and that the letter was in *The Times* on that date? He mentions many other specifics: dates, times, places, full names, prices and distances. What is the effect of so much specific information?

Style

19 *The Lost Special* is written as an impersonal report, yet the effect on the reader is that of an exciting story. The use of the different texts provides variety that helps to maintain the pace and create excitement.

Look at the different texts. Which are most formal? Which are less formal?

a) the main body of the story, written as a report
b) Herbert de Lernac's statement to the French police (translated)
c) Inspector Collins's official report
d) James McPherson's letter to his wife
e) the letter from *The Times*, dated 3rd July
f) the telegrams from various stationmasters along the route

20 Choose adjectives from the box to describe the various texts:

objective	pompous	to the point	ornate
personal	dramatic	wordy	impersonal

21 Read the first two paragraphs of the story again. Notice the number of passive structures here, such as 'No importance was attached to the fact at the time'. What effect do these passive structures have on style?

22 Look at the passage starting: 'The two officials stared at each other in amazement', where Mr Bland and his colleague discuss the information from the telegrams [page 27]. How does this differ in style from a report? Why does the writer recount their conversation word for word?

23 Now read the first two paragraphs of Herbert de Lernac's statement [page 34]. Notice how he talks in the first person about himself and addresses his intended readers as 'messieurs'. He gives warnings and exclamations. Notice, too, how different punctuation is used from the rest of the story. How does this change in style affect your understanding of de Lernac's character?

Guidance to the above literary terms, answer keys to all the exercises and activities, plus a wealth of other reading-practice material, can be found at: www.macmillanenglish.com/readers.

The Mysterious Card
by Cleveland Moffett

About the author

Cleveland Moffett was an author and journalist who wrote several novels and short stories, as well as numerous magazine articles, which were always on popular topics. Later in his life he wrote plays and screenplays for Hollywood. He is best known for the short story you are about to read and his 1909 novel, *Through the Wall*.

Cleveland Langston Moffett was born in upper New York State in 1863. After graduating from Yale University, he was taken on as a journalist for the *New York Herald* from 1883 until 1892. For the next few years he wrote for various magazines and newspapers on a wide range of topics. Many of his articles reveal a fascination for science and technology, writing about new inventions such as the Rontgen ray, airship, and horseless carriage (or x-ray, plane and car, as we now know them). He also wrote about real-life crimes solved by the Pinkerton Detective Agency, the largest private security and detective agency in the world at the time. In 1897, he published these stories as a collection, *True Detective Stories*. Similarly, in 1901, he collected together articles that he had written for children called *Careers of Danger and Daring* about people with dangerous jobs. His special skill as a writer was in capturing the excitement of the United States just as it was becoming the world power it is today.

His career continued to develop during the first decade of the twentieth century. He made a name as a successful novelist and playwright. His first novel, *A King in Rags*, shows his concern for social justice, but his politics became even more important when World War One broke out in 1914. Moffett became a supporter of patriotism, advocating a strong American foreign policy. In his writing and in public speeches he held the view that the United States should prepare for military action against its enemies. He visited the front in Europe, after which he wrote a fictitious account of the invasion of America by Germany.

His work as a journalist took him to Europe for several years as foreign correspondent for various New York newspapers, and many of his works, including *The Mysterious Card*, are set in France. *The Mysterious Card* is not his only mystery; *The Land of Mystery* is a novel set in Egypt and includes supernatural elements such as characters with telepathic powers. Another form of mystery, the detective novel, is represented in his work in *Through the Wall*, which is also set in Paris and shares many of the themes of *The Mysterious Card*.

Cleveland Moffett died in 1926 aged 63. He was a busy and successful author in his day, at the turn of the twentieth century, and wrote in an accessible style about popular topics. Apart from this story, though, his work is largely forgotten today.

About the story

The Mysterious Card was published in *The Black Cat* magazine in February of 1896. The card's mystery aroused intense interest among his readers, so a year later Moffett wrote a sequel, *The Mysterious Card Unveiled*, to satisfy their curiosity. One publishing company sold both stories together; you had to break a paper seal in order to read the second story. The publisher cleverly promised a refund if the books were returned to the bookshop with the seal unbroken. Despite the interest, many fans of *The Mysterious Card* were unhappy with the solution given in the second story because it relied on supernatural powers and evil spirits – elements that had been absent in the original. One reader, Edward D. Hoch, was so dissatisfied that he wrote his own version in 1975, named *The Spy and the Mysterious Card*, which gives a more realistic explanation for what happens.

Background information

Americans in Europe

For wealthy society in the United States in the late nineteenth century, visiting Europe was seen as an important part of a person's cultural education. Another reason for crossing the Atlantic Ocean was to do business. There were frequent ocean crossings by 'steamers', large steam boats, from New York to ports in Britain and the rest of Europe. Passengers who could afford it travelled in luxury; they had their own 'staterooms', luxury cabins with their own bathroom. The journey was typically completed in little more than a week. The two continents had never been so close.

Most Americans landed first in Great Britain before travelling on to mainland Europe. French and Italian society, in particular, were held in very high regard as cultures to learn from. Meanwhile, Europeans often expressed a feeling of superiority to their American 'Yankee' neighbours, who some saw as uncultured. But Americans also got frustrated with the old-fashioned and outdated ways of Europe. For despite this admiration for 'old' Europe, America was quickly becoming the powerful nation that it is today; it was proud of its 'newness' and Americans embraced modernity whole-heartedly.

Summary

It may help you to know something about what happens in the story before you read it. Don't worry, this summary does *not* tell you how the story ends!

Richard Burwell is on a trip to Europe with his family. His wife and daughter stay in London while he continues on to Paris alone. He decides to see a show at the famous music hall, the Folies Bergère. There he is given a card by an extremely beautiful woman who neither speaks to him nor pays him any further attention.

The card has some writing on it, but it is in French, so when Burwell returns to his hotel he asks the manager to translate it for him. However, as soon as the man reads the card, he demands that Burwell leave the hotel immediately. Shocked and angry, Burwell is forced to find a different hotel. The same thing happens in the next hotel he stays in; the proprietor of the hotel refuses to let him stay after reading the card. Frustratingly, neither manager will explain to Burwell what the card says. Burwell visits an old friend from Boston who lives in Paris. This man, too, reacts in a similar way when he sees the card and makes an excuse why Burwell cannot stay for lunch.

Now he can think of nothing except the card. He tries various ways to make sense of what is happening to him, but only succeeds in being thrown in prison. Finally, Burwell leaves France after a representative from the US legation – what is nowadays called an embassy – manages to have him released by the French authorities.

However, leaving France does not prevent more terrible misfortunes happening to Burwell; the effects of the card on his life become more and more serious, first in London and then in New York. It seems that the whole world is working against him. He becomes totally obsessed with the card, which he hates but cannot throw away. Then, just one week after arriving home in New York, he sees someone who might put an end to his misery.

Pre-reading activities

Key vocabulary

This section will help you familiarize yourself with some of the more specific vocabulary used in the story. You may want to use it to help you before you start reading, or as a revision exercise after you have finished the story.

Ways of describing strong emotions

Burwell's trip to France quickly becomes a difficult one, full of emotion. The words in **bold** in the paragraphs below appear in the story and all express one of three emotions.

1 **Which emotion is expressed in each paragraph? Anger, surprise or confusion?**

a) Karen **started** when she saw him enter the room. A look of **astonishment** crossed her face. 'I thought you were in …' she said. He crossed over to her and reached out to touch her. 'I just **can't believe my eyes** … you're here'. She jumped into his arms.

b) Although the accident caused no deaths, airline officials are **mystified** as to why the plane should have broken in two on take-off. One **bewildered** passenger was found walking across the runway wearing his life jacket.

c) 'This is an **outrage**!' the customer shouted, but there was no persuading the shop assistant to exchange the broken camera. **Indignant**, he filled in the complaints book and **stormed** out of the shop, with his head held high but still clearly **piqued**.

2 Check your answers by looking at the definitions.

astonishment (n) very great surprise
bewildered (adj) confused and not certain what to do
indignant (adj) angry because of an unfair situation or someone's unfair behaviour
mystify (v) if someone or something mystifies you, you cannot understand or explain it
outrage (n) an event or action that makes you feel extremely angry and upset
piqued (adj) slightly annoyed and offended
start (v) to move suddenly because you are afraid or surprised by something
storm (v) to go somewhere very quickly because you are angry or upset
I can't believe my eyes PHRASE used for saying that you find something that you see difficult to believe

3 Use words or phrases in 2 to complete the sentences. Make any necessary changes.

1 'What we are doing to the environment is an _____!' exclaimed one campaigner.
2 Furious that no one believed him, he _____ out of the room.
3 She _____ when she saw the spider hanging just centimetres from her nose.
4 The guests were all so _____ at the poor service they received that they refused to pay.
5 I wasn't expecting any reward at all, so imagine my _____ when a cheque for $500 came in the mail!
6 When the old woman woke up she was in a hospital bed. She had no memory of getting there. _____, she got out of bed and looked for her clothes.
7 There were wild bulls running down the street! I _____!

Descriptive language

The plot is driven by the way the characters react to the card and the dramatic events that unfold. Moffett expresses these reactions in a number of ways: by reporting what they say, describing how they speak and depicting their physical movements.

Reporting verbs

A lot of the action is conveyed through the conversations that Burwell has with other characters. Moffett uses reporting verbs to describe their emotions and reactions.

4 Look at the reporting verbs in bold in these extracts. Match them with their definitions below.

… growing tender at the sight of her distress, he took her hand in his and **begged** *her to be calm.*

Now Burwell grew angry, and he **declared** *heatedly that if he wasn't wanted in this hotel there were others in Paris where he would be welcome.*

'Then, for God's sake, tell me, what does it all mean?' he **gasped***, quivering with excitement.*

'Do you remember seeing me a month ago?' He came closer to hear her, she was so weak. 'Yes,' she **murmured***.*

Burwell **pleaded** *to know what it was about; but it changed nothing. The Secretary positively refused to throw any light on the causes of this monstrous injustice.*

1 to say something in a formal or impressive way
2 to ask for something in an urgent or emotional way
3 to ask for something in a way that shows you want it very much
4 to say something in a very quiet voice
5 to say something suddenly with a sharp intake of air because you are shocked

5 Choose the most appropriate reporting verb to complete the sentences.

1 'Please don't tell my mum and dad about it,' he **pleaded/declared** desperately, 'I swear I won't do it again'.
2 'Don't look now, but that man you spoke to last night is right behind you,' her friend **reasoned/murmured** quietly.
3 'There's nothing wrong with taking a little money, really. I mean, I'm going to give it back as soon as I get paid. Please don't tell anyone!' he **reasoned/begged**.
4 She dived into the lake at last. 'Oh, my goodness! It's cold', she **declared/gasped**.
5 'That was a silly move, taking my queen. I've got check mate in two … three moves,' **declared/murmured** Uncle Peter loudly and confidently.

Adverbs of manner

Moffett uses a number of adverbs to describe the way people in the story behave and speak.

6 Choose an adverb from the box to complete the sentences. Choose the correct position.

> **deftly** moving quickly and with skill
> **heatedly** if you talk heatedly, you get angry and excited
> **solemnly** in a serious and sad way
> **sternly** in a serious and severe way
> **strikingly** attracting your interest or attention because of some unusual feature

1 He was dressed in an electric-blue suit.
2 There were a few cries from the crowd as the funeral train marched through the town.
3 As they argued more and more, so the noise level rose until, by the end, it was mostly shouting.
4 She stepped over the stones in the stream.
5 The detective spoke to the officers about the dangers of confronting this man alone.

Verbs describing movement

Strong emotions are conveyed in the story by dramatic movement. Moffett creates variety in the reading experience by using different verbs that are almost synonymous.

7 Group the verbs in bold according to their similar meanings.

Group 1 – verbs which mean to shake with small quick movements, sometimes because of fear, nerves or excitement

Group 2 – verbs which mean to hold, or take and hold someone or something tightly with your hand

1 He **clasped** the tortured man's hand in his with a strong grip.
2 The sunken eyes **fluttered**, forced themselves open, and stared in stony amazement at the fatal card.
3 He deeply regretted that he had not torn up the miserable card … He even **seized** it, prepared to strip it into fragments.
4 He rushed on shore and **grasped** the hand of his partner.
5 The **trembling** lips moved noiselessly, as if in an attempt to speak.
6 A suggestion of a smile **flickered** across the woman's face.

7 Frantically **snatching** the card from its envelope, he held it close to the woman's face.

8 He leaned over the bed, **clutching** in one hand an envelope containing the mysterious card.

9 'Then, for God's sake, tell me, what does it all mean?' he gasped, **quivering** with excitement.

Using French words

As the story is set, mainly, in France, it contains quite a few French words. Readers who don't speak French must guess their meaning from context.

8 What do you think the French words in bold might mean? Choose the correct English words from the list below.

Calling a (1) fiacre, he drove to the Hôtel Continental, where he was staying.

'Now I understand why my (2) confrère refused to serve you. I regret, (3) monsieur, but I shall be obliged to do as he did.'

With his luggage on the carriage, he ordered the (4) cocher to drive directly there

… he saw no other course than to lay the problem before a detective agency. He accordingly put his case in the hands of an (5) agent de la sûreté who was recommended as a competent and trustworthy man.

a) carriage driver

b) policeman

c) horse-drawn cab, or taxi

d) sir

e) colleague

Main themes

Before you read the story, you may want to think about some of its main themes. The questions will help you think about the story as you are reading it for the first time. There is more discussion of the main themes in the *Literary analysis* section after the story.

Lost in translation

The main character, Richard Burwell, is a man abroad in a culture that is not his own. The writer says that when he tries to read French it is 'all Greek to him' (if someone says: 'It's all Greek to me', they mean that they cannot understand a single word). Burwell is the only person in the story who does not speak French and this puts him at a great disadvantage. The first sentence of the story makes this very clear when it states that he regrets not learning French. The story tries to capture the feelings of helplessness and total dependence on others that being in a foreign country can create. Once, Burwell uses a dictionary: he 'tried to pick out the meaning word by word, but failed'. The story raises an important question about languages: is it enough to translate the words alone, or are there cultural elements that don't cross linguistic barriers?

French was the language for international relations and diplomacy at the time of the story, and being able to speak it showed a level of education and culture that opened many doors socially and professionally. Burwell is a successful businessman in his home country. There he has no problems communicating, but in Paris he becomes lost.

9 As you read the story, ask yourself:

a) In what ways is he lost in Paris?
b) Why does the dictionary not help him?
c) What else could he have tried in order to understand better?

Curiosity and obsession

Throughout the story Burwell asks the same question in different ways and to different people: 'What does it mean?' What starts as mild curiosity quickly develops into something obsessive.

10 As you read the story, ask yourself:

a) Why is Burwell initially interested in the card?
b) Does his interest change as the story progresses?
c) At what point would you say his curiosity about the card becomes an obsession?
d) Why does he not simply throw the card away?

⑦ The Mysterious Card

by Cleveland Moffett

Richard Burwell, of New York, will never **cease** to regret that the French language was not made a part of his education.

This is why:

On the second evening after Burwell arrived in Paris, feeling lonely without his wife and daughter, who were still visiting a friend in London, his mind naturally turned to the theatre. So, after consulting the daily amusement calendar, he decided to visit the Folies Bergère, which he had heard of as one of the notable sights. During an intermission he went into the beautiful garden, where gay[1] crowds were strolling among the flowers, and lights, and fountains. He had just seated himself at a little three-legged table, with a view to enjoying the novel scene, when his attention was attracted by a lovely woman, gowned strikingly, though in perfect taste, who passed near him, leaning on the arm of a gentleman. The only thing that he noticed about this gentleman was that he wore eye-glasses.

Now Burwell had never posed as a captivator of the fair sex[2], and could scarcely credit his eyes when the lady left the side of her escort and, turning back as if she had forgotten something, passed close by him, and deftly placed a card on his table. The card bore some French words written in purple ink, but, not knowing that language, he was unable to make out their meaning. The lady paid no further heed[3] to him, but, rejoining the gentleman with the eye-glasses, swept out of the place with the grace and dignity of a princess. Burwell remained staring at the card.

Needless to say, he thought no more of the performance or of the other attractions about him. Everything seemed flat and

1 *old-fashioned*: happy and excited
2 *old-fashioned*: women
3 *formal*: *to pay heed to something*: to give careful attention to something

tawdry compared with the radiant vision that had appeared and disappeared so mysteriously. His one desire now was to discover the meaning of the words written on the card.

Calling a fiacre[4], he drove to the Hôtel Continental, where he was staying. Proceeding directly to the office and taking the manager aside, Burwell asked if he would be kind enough to translate a few words of French into English. There were no more than twenty words in all.

'Why, certainly,' said the manager, with French politeness, and cast his eyes over the card. As he read, his face grew rigid with astonishment, and, looking at his questioner sharply, he exclaimed: 'Where did you get this, monsieur?

Burwell started to explain, but was interrupted by: 'That will do, that will do. You must leave the hotel.'

'What do you mean?' asked the man from New York, in amazement.

'You must leave the hotel now—tonight—without fail,' commanded the manager excitedly.

Now it was Burwell's turn to grow angry, and he declared heatedly that if he wasn't wanted in this hotel there were plenty of others in Paris where he would be welcome. And, with an assumption of dignity, but piqued at heart, he settled his bill, sent for his belongings, and drove up the Rue de la Paix to the Hôtel Bellevue, where he spent the night.

The next morning he met the proprietor, who seemed to be a good **fellow**, and, being inclined now to view the incident of the previous evening from its ridiculous side, Burwell explained what had befallen[5] him, and was pleased to find a sympathetic listener.

'Why, the man was a fool,' declared the proprietor. 'Let me see the card; I will tell you what it means.' But as he read, his face and manner changed instantly.

'This is a serious matter,' he said sternly. 'Now I understand why my confrère[6] refused to entertain you. I regret, monsieur,

4 French: horse-drawn cab or taxi
5 *literary*: if something unpleasant befalls you, it happens to you
6 French: colleague

but I shall be obliged to do as he did.'

'What do you mean?'

'Simply that you cannot remain here.'

With that he turned on his heel, and the indignant guest could not prevail upon[7] him to give any explanation.

'We'll see about this,' said Burwell, thoroughly angered.

It was now nearly noon, and the New Yorker remembered an engagement to lunch with a friend from Boston, who, with his family, was stopping at the Hôtel de l'Alma. With his luggage on the carriage, he ordered the cocher[8] to drive directly there, determined to take counsel[9] with his countryman before selecting new **quarters**. His friend was highly indignant when he heard the story – a fact that gave Burwell no little comfort, knowing, as he did, that the man was accustomed to foreign ways from long residence abroad.

'It is some silly mistake, my dear fellow; I wouldn't pay any attention to it. Just have your luggage taken down and stay here. It is a nice, homelike place, and it will be very **jolly**, all being together. But, first, let me prepare a little 'nerve settler' for you.'

After the two had lingered a moment over their Manhattan cocktails, Burwell's friend excused himself to call the ladies. He had proceeded only two or three steps when he turned, and said: 'Let's see that mysterious card that has raised all this **row**.'

He had scarcely withdrawn it from Burwell's hand when he started back, and exclaimed: –

'Great God, man! Do you mean to say – this is simply – '

Then, with a sudden movement of his hand to his head, he left the room.

He was gone perhaps five minutes, and when he returned his face was white.

'I am awfully sorry,' he said nervously, 'but the ladies tell me the – that is, my wife – she has a frightful headache. You will have to excuse us from the lunch.'

---

7 *formal phrasal verb*: to ask or persuade someone to do something
8 French: carriage driver
9 *uncommon, formal*: if you take counsel with someone, you ask for their advice

Instantly realizing that this was only a **flimsy** pretense[10], and deeply hurt by his friend's behaviour, the mystified man arose at once and left without another word. He was now determined to solve this mystery at any cost. What could be the meaning of the words on that **infernal** piece of pasteboard?

Profiting by his humiliating experiences, he took good care not to show the card to any one at the hotel where he now established himself, – a comfortable little place near the Grand Opera House.

All through the afternoon he thought of nothing but the card, and turned over in his mind various ways of learning its meaning without getting himself into further trouble. That evening he went again to the Folies Bergère in hope of finding the mysterious woman, for he was now more than ever anxious to discover who she was. It even occurred to him that she might be one of those beautiful Nihilist[11] conspirators, or, perhaps, a Russian spy, such as he had read of in novels. But he failed to find her, either then or on the three subsequent evenings which he passed in the same place. Meanwhile the card was burning in his pocket like a hot coal. He dreaded the thought of meeting anyone that he knew, while this horrible cloud hung over him. He bought a French-English dictionary and tried to pick out the meaning word by word, but failed. It was all Greek to him. For the first time in his life, Burwell regretted that he had not studied French at college.

After various vain attempts to either solve or forget the torturing **riddle**, he saw no other course than to lay the problem before a detective agency. He accordingly put his case in the hands of an agent de la sûreté[12] who was recommended as a competent and trustworthy man. They had a talk together in a private room, and, of course, Burwell showed the card. To his relief, his adviser at least showed no sign of taking offence. Only he did not and would not explain what the words meant.

10 American spelling, in British English the spelling is *pretence*
11 belonging to a nineteenth century Russian political movement that rejected all authorities such as the church and government
12 a member of the French police force

'It is better,' he said, 'that monsieur should not know the nature of this document for the present. I will do myself the honour to call upon monsieur tomorrow at his hotel, and then monsieur shall know everything.'

'Then it is really serious?' asked the unfortunate man.

'Very serious,' was the answer.

The next twenty-four hours Burwell passed in a fever of anxiety. As his mind **conjured up** one fearful possibility after another he deeply regretted that he had not torn up the miserable card at the start. He even seized it, – prepared to strip it into fragments, and so end the whole affair. And then his Yankee stubbornness again asserted itself, and he determined to see the thing out, come what might[13].

'After all,' he reasoned, 'it is no crime for a man to pick up a card that a lady drops on his table.'

Crime or no crime, however, it looked very much as if he had committed some grave offence when, the next day, his detective drove up in a carriage, accompanied by a uniformed official, and requested the astounded American to accompany them to the police headquarters.

'What for?' he asked.

'It is only a formality,' said the detective; and when Burwell still protested the man in uniform remarked; 'You'd better come quietly, monsieur; you will have to come, anyway.'

An hour later, after severe cross-examination by another official, who demanded many facts about the New Yorker's age, place of birth, residence, occupation, etc., the bewildered man found himself in the Conciergerie[14] prison. Why he was there or what was about to befall him Burwell had no means of knowing; but before the day was over he succeeded in having a message sent to the American Legation, where he demanded immediate protection as a citizen of the United States. It was not until evening, however, that the Secretary of Legation, a **consequential** person, called at the prison. There followed a stormy interview, in which the prisoner used some strong

13 *formal*: despite anything that might happen, normally, *come what may*
14 a famous prison where many people were executed during the French Revolution

language, the French officers **gesticulated** violently and talked very fast, and the Secretary calmly listened to both sides, said little, and smoked a good cigar.

'I will lay your case before the American minister,' he said as he rose to go, 'and let you know the result tomorrow.'

'But this is an outrage. Do you mean to say – '

Before he could finish, however, the Secretary, with a strangely suspicious glance, turned and left the room.

That night Burwell slept in a cell.

The next morning he received another visit from the **non-committal** Secretary, who informed him that matters had been arranged, and that he would be set at liberty forthwith.

'I must tell you, though,' he said, 'that I have had great difficulty in accomplishing this, and your liberty is granted only on condition that you leave the country within twenty-four hours, and never under any conditions return.'

Burwell stormed, raged, and pleaded; but it availed[15] nothing. The Secretary was inexorable[16], and yet he positively refused to throw any light upon the causes of this monstrous injustice.

'Here is your card,' he said, handing him a large envelope closed with the seal of Legation. 'I advise you to burn it and never refer to the matter again.'

That night the **ill-fated** man took the train for London, his heart consumed by hatred for the whole French nation, together with a burning desire for vengeance. He wired[17] his wife to meet him at the station, and for a long time debated with himself whether he should at once tell her the sickening truth. In the end he decided that it was better to keep silent. No sooner, however, had she seen him than her woman's instinct told her that he was labouring under some mental strain. And he saw in a moment that to withhold from her his burning secret was impossible, especially when she began to talk of the trip they had planned through France. Of course no trivial reason would satisfy her for his refusal to make this trip, since they had been

15 *formal, unusual*: if something doesn't avail, it doesn't help or benefit
16 *formal, unusual*: impossible to persuade and refusing to change a decision
17 sent a telegram

looking forward to it for years; and yet it was impossible now for him to set foot on French soil.

So he finally told her the whole story, she laughing and weeping in turn. To her, as to him, it seemed incredible that such overwhelming disasters could have grown out of so small a cause, and, being a fluent French scholar, she demanded a sight of the **fatal** piece of pasteboard. In vain her husband tried to divert her by proposing a trip through Italy. She would consent to nothing until she had seen the mysterious card which Burwell was now convinced he ought long ago to have destroyed. After refusing for a while to let her see it, he finally **yielded**. But, although he had learned to dread the consequences of showing that cursed card, he was little prepared for what followed. She read it, turned pale, gasped for breath, and nearly fell to the floor.

'I told you not to read it,' he said; and then, growing tender at the sight of her distress, he took her hand in his and begged her to be calm. 'At least tell me what the thing means,' he said. 'We can bear it together; you surely can trust me.'

But she, as if stung by rage, pushed him from her and declared, in a tone such as he had never heard from her before, that never, never again would she live with him. 'You are a monster!' she exclaimed. And those were the last words he heard from her lips.

Failing utterly in all efforts at reconciliation, the half-crazed man took the first steamer for New York, having suffered in scarcely a fortnight more than in all his previous life. His whole pleasure trip had been ruined, he had failed to consummate[18] important business arrangements, and now he saw his home broken up and his happiness ruined. During the voyage he scarcely left his stateroom, but lay there prostrated[19] with agony. In this black despondency the one thing that sustained him was the thought of meeting his partner, Jack Evelyth, the friend of his boyhood, the sharer of his success, the bravest, most loyal

18 *formal*: to complete something, especially a business deal or agreement
19 *formal*: if you are prostrated with something such as pain or sadness, it completely
   takes control of you

fellow in the world. In the face of even the most damning circumstances, he felt that Evelyth's **rugged** common sense would evolve some way of escape from this hideous nightmare. Upon landing at New York he hardly waited for the gang-plank to be lowered before he rushed on shore and grasped the hand of his partner, who was waiting on the **wharf**.

'Jack,' was his first word, 'I am in dreadful trouble, and you are the only man in the world who can help me.'

An hour later Burwell sat at his friend's dinner table, talking over the situation. Evelyth was all kindness, and several times as he listened to Burwell's story his eyes filled with tears.

'It does not seem possible, Richard,' he said, 'that such things can be; but I will stand by you; we will fight it out together. But we cannot strike in the dark. Let me see this card.'

'There is the damned[20] thing,' Burwell said, throwing it on the table.

Evelyth opened the envelope, took out the card, and fixed his eyes on the **sprawling** purple characters.

'Can you read it?' Burwell asked excitedly.

'Perfectly,' his partner said. The next moment he turned pale, and his voice broke. Then he clasped the tortured man's hand in his with a strong grip. 'Richard,' he said slowly, 'if my only child had been brought here dead it would not have caused me more sorrow than this does. You have brought me the worst news one man could bring another.'

His agitation and genuine suffering affected Burwell like a death sentence.

'Speak, man,' he cried; 'do not spare me. I can bear anything rather than this awful uncertainty. Tell me what the card means.'

Evelyth took a swallow of brandy and sat with head bent on his clasped hands.

'No, I can't do it; there are some things a man must not do.'

Then he was silent again, his brows knitted[21]. Finally he said solemnly: –

20 *impolite*: used for emphasizing what you are saying, especially when you are annoyed about something
21 if you knit your brows, you move your eyebrows close together in an expression that shows you are worried, serious and thinking carefully

'No, I can't see any other way out of it. We have been true to each other all our lives; we have worked together and looked forward to never separating. I would rather fail and die than see this happen. But we have got to separate, old friend; we have got to separate.'

They sat there talking until late into the night. But nothing that Burwell could do or say availed against his friend's decision. There was nothing for it but that Evelyth should buy his partner's share of the business or that Burwell buy out the other. The man was more than fair in the financial proposition he made; he was generous, as he always had been, but his determination was inflexible; the two must separate. And they did.

With the old partner's desertion, it seemed to Burwell that the world was leagued against him. It was only three weeks from the day on which he had received the mysterious card; yet in that time he had lost all that he valued in the world, – wife, friends, and business. What next to do with the fatal card was the sickening problem that now possessed him.

He dared not show it; yet he dared not destroy it. He loathed it; yet he could not let it go from his possession. Upon returning to his house he locked the accursed[22] thing away in his safe as if it had been a package of dynamite or a bottle of deadly poison. Yet not a day passed that he did not open the drawer where the thing was kept and scan with loathing the mysterious purple **scrawl**.

In desperation he finally made up his mind to take up the study of the language in which the hateful thing was written. And still he dreaded the approach of the day when he should **decipher** its awful meaning.

One afternoon, less than a week after his arrival in New York, as he was crossing Twenty-third Street on the way to his French teacher, he saw a carriage rolling up Broadway. In the carriage was a face that caught his attention like a flash. As he looked again he recognized the woman who had been the cause of his undoing[23]. Instantly he sprang into another cab and ordered

22 *old-fashioned*: very annoying
23 *phrase*: if something or someone is the undoing of a person, they are the cause of the person's failure

the driver to follow after. He found the house where she was living. He called there several times; but always received the same reply, that she was too much engaged to see anyone. Next he was told that she was ill, and on the following day the servant said she was much worse. Three physicians had been summoned in consultation. He sought out one of these and told him it was a matter of life or death that he see this woman. The doctor was a kindly man and promised to assist him. Through his influence, it came about that on that very night Burwell stood by the bedside of this mysterious woman. She was beautiful still, though her face was worn with illness.

'Do you recognize me?' he asked tremblingly, as he leaned over the bed, clutching in one hand an envelope containing the mysterious card. 'Do you remember seeing me at the Folies Bergère a month ago?'

'Yes,' she murmured, after a moment's study of his face; and he noted with relief that she spoke English.

'Then, for God's sake, tell me, what does it all mean?' he gasped, quivering with excitement.

'I gave you the card because I wanted you to – to –'

Here a terrible spasm of coughing shook her whole body, and she fell back exhausted.

An agonizing despair tugged at Burwell's heart. Frantically snatching the card from its envelope, he held it close to the woman's face.

'Tell me! Tell me!'

With a supreme effort, the pale figure slowly raised itself on the pillow, its fingers clutching at the counterpane[24].

Then the sunken eyes fluttered – forced themselves open – and stared in stony amazement upon the fatal card, while the trembling lips moved noiselessly, as if in an attempt to speak. As Burwell, choking with eagerness, bent his head slowly to hers, a suggestion of a smile flickered across the woman's face. Again the mouth quivered, the man's head bent nearer and nearer to

24 *old-fashioned*: a top cover on a bed, used mainly for decoration

hers, his eyes riveted upon the lips. Then, as if to aid her in deciphering the mystery, he turned his eyes to the card.

With a cry of horror he sprang to his feet, his eyeballs starting from their sockets. Almost at the same moment the woman fell heavily upon the pillow.

Every **vestige** of the writing had faded! The card was blank!

The woman lay there dead.

Post-reading activities

Understanding the story

Use these questions to check that you have understood the story.

1 How long has Richard Burwell been in Paris?
2 Why does he decide to go to the Folies Bergère?
3 Why does he look at the woman?
4 What does he ask the manager of the hotel to do?
5 How does Burwell feel when he is forced to leave the first hotel?
6 How long does he stay in the second hotel?
7 Why does he believe his friend from Boston will be able to help him clear up the mystery?
8 His friend claims that his wife has a headache, which is why he cannot stay for lunch. Has she?
9 Who is the next person he shows the card to?
10 Why does the agent refuse to tell him what the card says until the following day?
11 Why does he decide not to destroy the card?
12 What does the American Legation secretary tell him to do after he is released from prison?
13 Why does he have to tell his wife what has happened to him even though he does not want to?
14 Who is Jack Evelyth?
15 In what way is Jack's reaction to the card similar to the others'? In what way is it different?
16 What is the result of the men's long conversation?
17 What does Burwell do with the card once he is in New York?
18 What else does Burwell decide to do now he is home?
19 Why does Burwell follow the woman?
20 What happens to the card at the end?

Language study

Grammar

Participle clauses

One of the features of Moffett's writing style is a great variety of sentence lengths. Some sentences are short and simple in order to create a dramatic effect:

> *That night Burwell slept in a cell.*
> *And those were the last words he heard from her lips.*
> *The woman lay there dead.*

Others are longer, describing multiple actions and carrying the story along:

> *Upon landing at New York he hardly waited for the gang-plank to be lowered before he rushed on shore and grasped the hand of his partner, who was waiting on the wharf.*

Moffett often uses participle clauses in his narration of the story e.g. *Upon landing at New York*. Here the clause replaces the past simple, which would be *After he landed at New York ...* It indicates that the landing in New York happened immediately before he rushed on shore. Participle clauses have other uses, too.

Form

Participle clauses are 'reduced clauses' – they contain a verb, but they do not normally contain a subject.

Present participle clauses (*-ing* clauses) replace verbs in the active.

> *Calling a fiacre, Burwell drove to the Hôtel Continental i.e. Burwell called a fiacre.*

Past participle clauses (*-ed* clauses) replace verbs in the passive.

> *The next day, his detective drove up in a carriage, accompanied by a uniformed official ... i.e. his detective was accompanied by the official.*

If no subject is mentioned in the participle clause, its subject must be the same as the main clause. However, the subject of the clause can be different from the main clause if it is placed before the participle:

> *That night **the ill-fated man** took the train for London, **his heart** consumed by hatred for the whole French nation.*

In this sentence the main subject is *the ill-fated man* but it is *his heart* which is *consumed by hatred*.

Prepositions can introduce participle clauses:

> So, **after consulting** the daily amusement calendar, he decided to visit the Folies Bergère.

The perfect aspect can be conveyed using the perfect participle:

> Burwell took the first steamer for New York, **having suffered** in a fortnight more than in all his previous life.

Use

Participle clauses are mainly used in writing. They allow the writer to shorten and combine sentences.

Participle clauses can be used to express why something happens (reason).

> The card bore some French words written in purple ink, but, **not knowing that language**, he was unable to make out their meaning. (Because he didn't know French, he was unable to make out their meaning)

They can be used to show that one action happens after another (time).

> **Frantically snatching the card from its envelope**, he held it close to the woman's face. (He snatched the card **then** held it close to her face)

They can also be used instead of relative clauses.

> His attention was attracted by a lovely woman, gowned strikingly (= who was gowned strikingly – a relative clause)

1 **Look at these two texts. Notice how, in the extract from the story, the sentences have been combined by participle clauses. Which words have been omitted or changed?**

He instantly realized that this was only a flimsy pretense. He was deeply hurt by his friend's behaviour. The mystified man arose at once and left without another word.

> Instantly **realizing** that this was only a flimsy pretense, and deeply **hurt** by his friend's behaviour, the mystified man arose at once and left without another word.

2 **Combine the sentences below using one or more participle clauses. More than one answer may be possible.**

1 Burwell proceeded directly to the office. He took the manager aside. He asked if he would be kind enough to translate a few words of French into English. [page 62]

2   He ordered the cocher to drive directly there. He was determined to take counsel with his countryman before he selected new quarters. [page 63]

3   So he finally told her the whole story. She laughed and wept in turn. [page 67]

4   The half-crazed man failed utterly in all efforts at reconciliation. He took the first steamer for New York. He had suffered in scarcely a fortnight more than in all his previous life. [page 67]

5   'There is the damned thing,' Burwell said. He threw it on the table. [page 68]

Compare your answers with the original sentences in the story.

No sooner, scarcely and just for dramatic narrative

Use

Moffett uses a range of adverbs to emphasize the dramatic nature of the action in the story. *No sooner, scarcely* and *just* are used to indicate that one action happens quickly after another action.

3   Which action happens first in each sentence?

*1 He had **just** seated himself at a little three-legged table, with a view to enjoying the novel scene, when his attention was attracted by a lovely woman.*

*2 He had **scarcely** withdrawn the card from Burwell's hand when he started back.*

*3 **No sooner**, however, had she seen him than her woman's instinct told her that he was labouring under some mental strain.*

Just, scarcely and *no sooner* modify verbs that describe actions that happen immediately before the action described in the main clause. *Just* is more common and less formal than *scarcely* and *no sooner*. All of them emphasize how quickly one action follows the other.

Form

4   Look at sentences 1–3 again. Notice the position of *just* and *scarcely* in the sentence. *No sooner* can also go in this position. Describe this position.

5   What tense is used in the time clause with the adverb?

6 **The two clauses in the sentences with *scarcely* and *just* are connected by the word *when*. What word connects the clauses in the sentence with *no sooner*?**

7 **Look at sentence 3 again. What do you notice about the word order?**

The adverbs *no sooner* and *scarcely*, and two other adverbs with the same use and form – *barely* and *hardly* – (but not *just*), can go at the start with this change of word order:

He had hardly shown the manager the card when he requested him to leave.

Hardly had he shown the manager the card when he requested him to leave.

The effect this has is to sound more formal and to emphasize the fact that the second action immediately follows the first.

Just as can go at the beginning of the sentence but there is no change of word order and no word like *when* or *than* connecting the two clauses:

Just as he had shown the manager the card, he requested him to leave.

8 **Combine the two sentences into one using the adverbs in bold. Place the adverb at the beginning of the sentence.**

1 She put the card on the table. She left. **no sooner**

....

2 He had finished packing his case. His cab arrived. **just as**

....

3 She read what was on the card. She pushed him away. **hardly**

....

4 He saw her face in the window of the carriage. He realized who she was. **scarcely**

....

5 The words faded from the card. He realized the woman was dead. **barely**

....

Vocabulary

Use of epithets

An epithet is an adjective which accompanies a person or thing to describe it but is not essential to the meaning of the sentence. It decorates the noun rather than introducing new information about it:

*That night the **ill-fated** man took the train for London*

Compare with the less dramatic alternative:

That night Burwell took the train for London

In the following example, Moffett could have just said 'the card':

*He had learned to dread the consequences of showing that **cursed** card.*

Moffett uses epithets for both the card and Burwell, not just decoratively, but to convey the frustration that Burwell feels.

*'There is the **damned** thing,' Burwell said, throwing it on the table.*

9 **Group the adjectives according to whether they could be used to describe a) the card b) the man c) either:**

accursed

cursed

damned

fatal

half-crazed

hateful

ill-fated

infernal

miserable

mysterious

tortured

unfortunate

Literary analysis

Plot

1 List the main events in the plot. How many people does Burwell show the card to?

2 Write a one-sentence summary of the plot.

3 Think about the characters' different reactions to seeing the card. Who …
   a) rejects him violently?
   b) says how sorry he is to reject him?
   c) tells him to leave because of the seriousness of the matter?
   d) consults with someone else before making excuses?
   e) tells him to leave without an explanation?
   f) remains calm but sets a trap for him?

4 What do the reactions indicate about the contents of the card?

5 What could Burwell have done to prevent the terrible events that happen to him? Why didn't he do this?

6 Traditional stories of this type end with the mystery being explained. Did you expect to discover the secret of the card at the end of the story? Do you think it is a strength or a weakness that the writing on the card remains a mystery? Why?

7 What do you think is the secret of the card?
   (If you are interested in learning more about the story, you can look for the sequel, *The Mysterious Card Unveiled*.)

Character

8 What do you know about Richard Burwell? What can you guess about his age, educational background, class, family and profession? Choose three adjectives to describe him.

9 Do you like him, care about him, or share his emotions in any way? Why/Why not?

10 Do you think his decision not to throw the card away is understandable?

11 What do we know about the mysterious woman? What is she like at the beginning of the story? What is she like at the end? Does she remind you of any characters you have read about or seen in films? Does she conform to any stereotypes?

12 Apart from Burwell and the mysterious woman, which character or characters interest you most? Why?

Narration

13 Who tells the story? From whose point of view is it told? Whose thoughts and feelings are described? And whose are not?

14 Look at the extract below. The question is an example of 'interior monologue', when we share the thoughts of one of the characters. Why does Moffett let Burwell's voice interrupt here?

> *He was now determined to solve this mystery at any cost. What could be the meaning of the words on that infernal piece of pasteboard?*

15 Look at the second extract below. How does Moffett tell us Burwell's thoughts this time? What does the use of punctuation indicate?

> *And then his Yankee stubbornness again asserted itself, and he determined to see the thing out, come what might.*
>
> *'After all,' he reasoned, 'it is no crime for a man to pick up a card that a lady drops on his table.'*

16 Find two other instances in the text of interior monologue. How does this help us identify with Burwell?

17 Think about how differently the story would have been told if it had been told by Burwell's friend Jack. How would it differ if his wife had told it? Would it have been very different if it had been told in the first person?

Style

18 What is the effect of including French words in the story?

19 Compare Burwell's two meetings with the mysterious woman, at the beginning of the story and in the final scene. Describe the atmosphere in the two scenes. How is the final scene different in atmosphere?

20 Notice how quickly their first meeting is described. She enters his life and disappears again just a few sentences later. Compare this with the final scene. Notice how Moffett focuses on the actions of Burwell and the mysterious woman in close detail. Why does he spend so long describing the final scene?

21 Imagine the story was made into a movie. What would the camera focus on in these final moments in the last scene?

22   Notice how suddenly the story ends, with no explanation or
     description of what happens after the woman dies. Look at the
     last three sentences. Notice how Moffett uses short sentences. Try
     reading the paragraph aloud. What effect does this create?

*Guidance to the above literary terms, answer keys to all the exercises and
activities, plus a wealth of other reading-practice material, can be found at:
www.macmillanenglish.com/readers.*

The Mildenhall Treasure
by Roald Dahl

About the author

Roald Dahl is one of the world's best-loved writers of children's literature. Many of his stories have been turned into films and cartoons, most famously *Charlie and the Chocolate Factory*. Dahl was most successful as a children's author but his *Tales of the Unexpected* for adults were very popular, too, as books and television dramatizations. One reason may be because the plain style he adopted for youngsters is equally attractive to adult readers. Another is certainly that his fantastic and sometimes frightening stories attract the curious child in all of us.

Dahl was born in Wales in 1916 to Norwegian parents. Sadly, his eldest sister died when she was just seven. Their father became so depressed that when he got pneumonia a few months later, he refused to fight the disease and he died, too. Roald was just three years old. Tragically, forty-two years later, Dahl's own daughter died of measles, also aged seven.

Dahl writes about his schooldays in his autobiography, *Boy*. He had a horrible time and was appalled by the cruelty of the teachers. Perhaps the unfair treatment he received as a child is one reason that many of his stories end with punishment for the villains, who are always adults, and justice for the weak and powerless, usually children.

When the war broke out in 1939, Dahl joined the Royal Air Force and flew fighter planes in Africa. On his first flight into enemy territory he had to crash land and was very nearly killed, but several months later he was flying again, this time in Greece and Palestine. However, the injury he had suffered to his head in the crash eventually prevented him from flying, so he was sent to the USA as an air attaché, a kind of diplomat, for the RAF.

It was here in America that he discovered a talent for writing. His first story, *Shot down in Libya*, all about his crash in the desert, was published in the *Saturday Evening Post* in 1942. He continued to write for American magazines for the rest of the war and, even after he returned to Britain, stories of his, such as *The Mildenhall Treasure*, were still published in the USA. Back in England he published his first collection of short stories, *Over to You*, and went on to write several more books. All of his writing had been for adults: stories of strange crimes and fantasy, attracting the attention of Alfred Hitchcock, among others. In America in 1961 he hosted a popular television show, *Way Out*. Later he appeared on television in Britain in a similar show, *Tales of the Unexpected*, which dramatized his own mystery stories.

In 1957 his daughter was born, and three years later a son, and it wasn't long before he started writing for children. *James and the Giant Peach* was published in 1962. From this point on, the majority of Dahl's work was directed at younger readers. In fact, he wrote so much children's fiction that after he died in 1990, new books continued to be published. And they keep appearing in film adaptations. *Charlie and the Chocolate Factory* and *Fantastic Mr Fox* have both been adapted for cinema, with Willy Wonka played by Johnny Depp and George Clooney lending his voice to Mr Fox.

Dahl once said: 'If my books can help children become readers, then I feel I have accomplished something important'. His books have sold over 100 million copies in more than 50 languages.

About the story

Dahl stayed away from real-life stories for most of his career. *The Mildenhall Treasure* is unusual, then, because it deals with the true story of how Roman treasure was discovered in a field in eastern England. It was first published in the *Saturday Evening Post* in 1947. In 1977 Dahl reprinted the story in a collection called *The Wonderful Story of Henry Sugar and Six Others*. Dahl introduces the new edition with a note that gives more information about how the story came to be written, and places Dahl himself as a character in the story. In the note he says that he wrote it because 'True stories about … really big treasure send shivers of electricity all the way down my legs to the soles of my feet'.

Background information

The Romans in Britain

At its height, the Roman Empire included most of Europe and the southern coast of the Mediterranean Sea. In AD 43 the Romans extended their empire by invading 'Britannia'. They ended up staying for 400 years. In that time they built towns and roads, traded with the

Britons and settled down with their wives and families. The wealthy Roman officers built villas, or large houses, for their families and brought from Italy their expensive possessions and their religions, both the traditional Roman religion and later, the Christian religion. Some of the Roman gods are mentioned in the story.

But the Romans failed to take over the whole of Britain, and were frequently invaded by the Scots and the Picts, tribes from the north. They finally abandoned Britain and returned to Italy in AD 410 when Italy itself was being invaded; the soldiers were needed at home to defend the mother land.

The Mildenhall Treasure

If you ever visit the British Museum in London or look online, you will see the fabulous treasure that this story is all about. Nothing like it had ever been discovered in Britain before. Because of its unusually fine quality, many experts at the time doubted whether such fine silver would have existed in this distant part of the Roman Empire.

In fact, there has been a lot of mystery surrounding the find. Some argued that the treasure could not have come from the field in Mildenhall because none of the pieces show any dents or other damage from having been discovered with heavy farm machinery. Also, after the discovery was made public, experts explored the area where the treasure was reported to have been found but there was no sign of digging and they couldn't find any other objects. These question marks about the discovery helped to generate different theories about the treasure's origins. One theory suggested that the treasure was taken from a site in Italy during World War II, brought back to the American military air base in Mildenhall and buried in the ground nearby!

The Fens

The story is set in Suffolk, a rural area in the east of England also known as 'the Fens'. The Fens are very flat and windy, which makes them good for farming cereal crops like wheat and barley. Barley is an important cereal in Britain for making beer and whisky as well as food. The area is also suitable for root vegetables, things like potatoes and sugar beet which grow under the ground. However, it is quite a cold and lonely place to live. During the war it was difficult to import food from other countries, so the Fens became very important for providing Britain with food.

Summary

It may help you to know something about what happens in the story before you read it. Don't worry, this summary does *not* tell you how the story ends!

The writer, Roald Dahl, was reading the newspaper one morning in 1947 when he noticed a story about some Roman treasure that had been discovered in a field in Suffolk. Excited by a possible story about lost treasure, he jumped in his car and travelled to Mildenhall, a morning's drive away. There he found and spoke to the man who first found the treasure, Gordon Butcher. He explained that if the man told him the story, he would write it and try to sell it and he would share any money he made with Butcher. This is Butcher's story.

Butcher was a ploughman, a farmer who prepares the earth for new plants and looks after the fields. In 1942, in the middle of the war, he had been asked by a man called Ford to plough a field (prepare it for planting crops). So he set off in his tractor and started ploughing the field. It was a very cold, windy day, with a possibility of snow. After a while his plough hit something in the earth. When he looked in the ground, he saw something large and made of metal. Feeling that this was strange, he left the field and went to find Ford at his house.

The two men returned to the field and Butcher showed Ford the object. They started digging. Quite soon they had pulled from the ground a large plate, then other plates and bowls, and still more objects kept coming. It began to snow, but they kept digging until they could see no more items. It was very cold. Ford sent Butcher home and took the objects back to his own house. And that was the last Butcher saw of the treasure for four years.

The war ended in 1945 and life returned to normal. The following year, Ford received a visit from an old acquaintance that brought the Mildenhall Treasure to the public's attention. But why had Ford taken the treasure in the first place? And why had he tried to keep it a secret for so long?

Pre-reading activities

Key vocabulary

This section will help you familiarize yourself with some of the more specific vocabulary used in the story. You may want to use it to help you before you start reading, or as a revision exercise after you have finished the story.

Archaeological exploration

1 **Look at the definitions of the following words connected with archaeology. Use the words to complete the text about the Mildenhall treasure. Make any necessary changes to the words.**

> **antiquities** objects or buildings that existed in ancient times and still exist
>
> **excavation** the process of digging in the ground to find things from the past
>
> **flint** hard grey stone that was used in the past for making tools
>
> **goblet** a metal or glass cup used in the past for drinking
>
> **hoard** a large amount of something that someone has saved or hidden somewhere
>
> **ladle** a large deep spoon with a long handle, used for serving liquids
>
> **pewter** a grey metal made by mixing lead and tin, used in the past for making plates, cups, and other objects
>
> **pottery** objects such as plates and cups that are made out of clay and baked in an oven so that they become hard
>
> **unearth** to find something that is buried in the ground
>
> **workmanship** the standard of someone's work, or the skill that they use in making something

Most archaeological 'digs', or (1) .... , will discover a few small objects: a brown piece of broken (2) .... , a stone arrowhead or other stone age tool made of (3) .... , a (4)........................ plate perhaps. When museums acquire pieces like this there is little excitement. But the Mildenhall Treasure is a huge (5) .... of many items of solid silver, which attracted attention from archaeologists and newspapers all over the world. There are large plates and bowls, personalized spoons, (6) .... for serving soup, (7) .... for drinking wine. All show (8) .... of the highest quality. What were such fine Roman (9) .... doing in a field in Suffolk a thousand miles from Italy? And were they really (10) .... by two farmers unaware of what they had found?

2 **Read the news article about a similar true story. Replace the phrases in bold with words from 1 above.**

Biggest archaeological find in Britain

Archaeologists in Hoxne have **found in the ground** a large amount of Roman coins, jewellery and tableware worth even more than the Mildenhall Treasure. Many of the items, such as bowls and **large spoons**, show beautiful **skill in making them**. The find was made when local farmer, Peter Whatling, asked a friend with a metal detector to help him look for a lost hammer. After digging up a **large amount** of coins and spoons, they contacted the Suffolk Archaeological Unit who completed the **digging operation** the following day. A spokesperson for the British Museum has said they are hoping to acquire the artefacts for their collection. The total expected value is approximately £1.75 million. Whatling offered the lost hammer to the museum for free.

Roman mythology

Roman gods and other mythological beings decorate the silver treasure. Here are some useful words.

Neptune the god of the sea

Bacchus the Roman name for Dionysus, the god of wine and revelry (parties!)

Pan the God of nature and the wild; half-man, half-goat, he plays the flute, or pipes

Maenads female followers of Bacchus, who love wine

satyrs male spirits with a similar appearance to Pan

nymphs young female spirits who love to 'gambol' (to run, jump, and play like a young child or animal)

Words describing the wind

The story takes place in January 1942. Winter in the Fens can be extremely cold and windy and Dahl describes the weather in great detail as a way of setting the scene.

3 **Look at the extracts below. All the words in bold refer to the wind in some way. Find the following:**

1 four verbs describing things that the wind does
2 two types of strong wind
3 two adjectives that describe strong wind
4 two verbs used here as nouns to describe noises that the wind makes
5 a word that means shelter
6 a synonym for anger

*His wife was out of bed now, standing beside him near the window, and the two of them were silent, listening to the **swish** and **whisk** of the icy wind as it came **sweeping** in over the fens.*

*He wheeled out the bike and mounted and began to ride down the middle of the narrow road, right into the face of the **gale**.*

*The wind **howled** around him and **snapped** at his coat.*

*The two men walked out of the shed into the **fierce**, ever-mounting **fury** of the wind.*

*He biked on down the road, pedaling hard against the **brutal** wind.*

*And all the while the **blizzard** **swirled** around them.*

*He found it and sat on the ground in the **lee** of one of the huge tractor wheels.*

Check your answers against the definitions

swish	to move quickly with a smooth sound, especially through the air
whisk	to move quickly
sweep	to move or spread quickly through an area, especially in a long wide curve
gale	a very strong wind
howl	to blow with a long loud sound
snap	to quickly move something so that it makes a short sound
fierce	very strong or severe
fury	a metaphor of anger describing the noise and force of extreme weather
lee	the side of a wall or other solid structure that provides shelter from the wind
brutal	extreme and cruel
blizzard	a storm with a lot of snow and strong winds
swirl	to move quickly in circles, or to make something move in this way

Adjectives to describe personality

Dahl contrasts the two main characters' personalities in terms of their knowledge and awareness of the world. Butcher is described as a simple person whereas Ford is described as rather clever.

4 Look at the definitions. Which adjectives do you think describe Butcher and which describe Ford?

---

artless very sincere and willing to trust other people

canny good at judging situations, especially in business, and careful not to be tricked

crafty good at getting what you want, especially in a slightly dishonest way

cunning using your intelligence to get what you want, especially by tricking or cheating people

foxy good at tricking or cheating people

ignorant not knowing something that you should know or need to know

learned knowing a lot about one or more subjects, especially academic subjects

simple-minded unable to understand difficult or complicated ideas

subtle indirect in a way that prevents people from noticing what you are trying to do

trusting willing to trust people, especially when it is not a sensible thing to do

---

Words connected with farming

5 Read the extracts. Match the words in bold with the definitions below.

*(a) Gordon Butcher was not an ordinary farm **laborer**. He owned his own **tractor**, and with this he **cultivated** other men's **plots**, **plowing** their fields and gathering their **harvests**. His wealth was in his small brick house with its small **yard** and **shed** that contained **spades** and shears and the other tools he needed to do his work, his two cows and his old, reliable tractor.*

1 to turn over the soil before putting seeds into it using a machine of the same name
2 the amount of a crop that is collected
3 an area without grass at the back of a small house
4 someone whose job involves hard physical work
5 a small building, usually made of wood, in which you store things
6 a vehicle used on farms to pull machines
7 grow crops or plants on a piece of land
8 a piece of land used for a particular purpose, such as growing plants

9 a tool used for digging with a handle and a flat metal part that you push into the earth with your foot

(b) *The field was knee-high with the **stubble** left from the previous year's harvest. Butcher got his tractor ready at the side of the field by a low **hedge**. He always **hitched** his **plow** to the tractor with a wooden **peg** so that if the plow **fouled** a root or a large stone, the peg would simply break at once, leaving the plow behind and saving the **plowshares** from serious damage.*

1 a piece of farm equipment used for turning over the soil before putting seeds into it
2 the blade of a plow (US spelling of *plough*)
3 an object used for fastening things together
4 to connect something such as a caravan to the back of a vehicle
5 to become stuck on something so that it cannot move
6 a line of bushes or small trees growing close together around a garden or field
7 the ends of plants that are left above ground after a farmer cuts a crop such as wheat or barley

6 Choose words from the extracts in 5 to complete the text.

Before the invention of the (1) .... , ploughing was a tiring task that would keep the ploughman and his horse or ox very busy for many weeks after the (2) .... had been collected. The plough was a simple tool that was (3) .... to the animal with a wooden harness, or 'yoke'. It had just one or two metal (4) .... to turn the earth, unlike modern machines that have between six and twelve. It was extremely slow.

A note about spelling

The Mildenhall Treasure was first written for the American market, so although Dahl was British he uses American English spelling in this story. However, in the 'note' that he added in the 1977 edition for the British market he uses British spelling; he talks about a *cheque*, which in American English is spelt *check*. Here are the other words in the story that differ in spelling between American and British English. Notice that some words with *-or* endings in American English spelling have *-our* endings in British English. Also, consonants at the end of unstressed syllables tend to be doubled in British English when followed by *-ed* or *-ing*.

American	British
plow	plough
plowman	ploughman
center	centre
archeologist, archeological	archaeologist, archaeological
gray	grey
kindhearted	kind-hearted
mantle	mantelpiece
laborer	labourer
parlor	parlour
favored	favoured
pedaling, pedaled	pedalling, pedalled
gamboled	gambolled
traveled	travelled
marvelous	marvellous

Main themes

Before you read the story, you may want to think about some of its main themes. The questions will help you think about the story as you are reading it for the first time. There is more discussion of the main themes in the *Literary analysis* section after the story.

Heroes and villains

A criticism of Dahl's work is that the characters are one-dimensional; the main characters have no faults and the villains are evil and deserve none of our sympathy. Dahl said:

'All good books have to have a mixture of extremely nasty people – which are always fun – and some nice people. In every story there has to be someone you can loathe (hate). *The fouler and more filthy a person is, the more fun it is to watch him getting scrunched* (destroyed).'

Dahl says in the introduction: 'I wrote the story as truthfully as I possibly could'. Clearly one reason for writing *The Mildenhall Treasure* was to tell the real story, but another reason was to tell a 'good' story, which, in Dahl's words means including a villain.

7 As you read, ask yourself:

a) Are all the characters in the story one-dimensional?
b) Who is the villain?
c) Do you think Dahl's portrait of the villain is fair?

Knowledge and innocence

Much of Dahl's work examines the theme of trust between people. Innocent people, who lack experience of the bad things people can do, tend to trust too much; a knowledge of life's hard lessons gives people reason not to put their faith in others. In order to succeed in life, Dahl seems to say, you need to lose your innocence and show some cunning. Some of his most popular characters are like this, such as Danny, in *Danny, the Champion of the World*, and the *Fantastic Mr Fox*, both of them are good at making clever plans and beating their enemies.

8 Think about these questions while you read the story:

a) Is being cunning a positive or negative trait in this story?
b) Who shows trust? Who shows a lack of trust?
b) Are you surprised by the trust, or lack of it, shown by the characters?

⊘ The Mildenhall Treasure

by Roald Dahl

A NOTE ABOUT THE NEXT STORY

In 1946, more than thirty years ago, I was still unmarried and living with my mother. I was making a fair income by writing two short stories a year. Each of them took four months to complete, and fortunately there were people both at home and abroad who were willing to buy them.

One morning in April of that year, I read in the newspaper about a remarkable find of Roman silver. It had been discovered three years before by a plowman near Mildenhall, in the county of Suffolk, but the discovery had for some reason been kept secret until then. The newspaper article said it was the greatest treasure ever found in the British Isles, and it had now been acquired by the British Museum. The name of the plowman was given as Gordon Butcher.

True stories about the finding of really big treasure send **shivers** of electricity all the way down my legs to the soles of my feet. The moment I read that story, I leaped up from my chair without finishing my breakfast and shouted goodbye to my mother and rushed out to my car. The car was a nine-year-old Wolseley[1], and I called it 'The Hard Black Slinker[2]'. It went well but not very fast.

Mildenhall was about one hundred twenty[3] miles from my home, a tricky cross-country trip along twisty roads and country lanes. I got there at lunchtime, and by asking at the local police station, I found the small house where Gordon Butcher lived with his family. He was at home having his lunch when I knocked on his door.

1 an old British car manufacturer that was very popular before the war
2 people used to give their cars names; *to slink* means to go somewhere slowly and quietly so that people will not notice you
3 *US English*: In UK English you write 'one hundred **and** twenty'

I asked him if he would mind talking to me about how he found the treasure.

'No, thank you,' he said. 'I've had enough of reporters. I don't want to see another reporter for the rest of my life.'

'I'm not a reporter,' I told him. 'I'm a short-story writer and I sell my work to magazines. They pay good money.' I went on to say that if he would tell me exactly how he found the treasure, then I would write a truthful story about it. And if I was lucky enough to sell it, I would split the money equally with him.

In the end, he agreed to talk to me. We sat for several hours in his little kitchen, and he told me an **enthralling** story. When he had finished, I paid a visit to the other man in the affair, an older fellow called Ford. Ford wouldn't talk to me and closed the door in my face. But by then I had my story and I set out for home.

The next morning, I went up to the British Museum in London to see the treasure that Gordon Butcher had found. It was fabulous. I got the shivers all over again just from looking at it.

I wrote the story as truthfully as I possibly could and sent it off to America. It was bought by the *Saturday Evening Post*, and I was paid well. When the money arrived, I sent exactly half of it to Gordon Butcher in Mildenhall.

Once week later, I received a letter from Mr. Butcher written upon[4] what must have been a page torn from a child's school exercise book. It said in part, '…you could have knocked me over with a feather[5] when I saw your cheque. It was lovely. I want to thank you …'

Here is the story almost exactly as it was written thirty years ago. I've changed it very little. I've simply toned down some of the more flowery passages and taken out a number of **superfluous** adjectives and unnecessary sentences.

———

Around seven o'clock in the morning, Gordon Butcher got out of bed and switched on the light. He walked barefoot to the window and drew back the curtains and looked out.

4 *formal*: on
5 if you say someone *could knock you over with a feather*, you are extremely surprised about something

This was January so it was still dark, but he could tell there hadn't been any snow in the night.

'That wind,' he said aloud to his wife. 'Just listen to that wind.'

His wife was out of bed now, standing beside him near the window, and the two of them were silent, listening to the swish and whisk of the icy wind as it came sweeping in over the fens.

'It's a nor'easter[6],' he said.

'There'll be snow for certain before nightfall,' she told him. 'And plenty of it.'

She was dressed before him, and she went into the next room and leaned over the cot of her six-year-old daughter and gave her a kiss. She called out a good morning to the two older children in the third room, then she went downstairs to make breakfast.

At a quarter to eight, Gordon Butcher put on his coat, his cap and his leather gloves and walked out the back door into the **bitter** early-morning winter weather. As he moved through the half-daylight over the yard to the shed where his bicycle stood, the wind was like a knife on his cheek. He wheeled out the bike and mounted and began to ride down the middle of the narrow road, right into the face of the gale.

Gordon Butcher was thirty-eight. He was not an ordinary farm laborer. He took orders from no man unless he wished. He owned his own tractor, and with this he plowed other men's fields and gathered other men's harvests under contract. His thoughts were only for his wife, his son, his two daughters. His wealth was in his small brick house, his two cows, his tractor, his skill as a plowman.

Gordon Butcher's head was very curiously shaped, the back of it protruding like the sharp end of an enormous egg, and his ears stuck out, and a front tooth was missing on the left side. But none of this seemed to matter very much when you met him face to face in the open air. He looked at you with steady blue eyes that were without any **malice** or cunning or greed. And the mouth didn't have those thin lines of **bitterness** around the edges that one so often sees on men who work the land and spend their days fighting the weather.

6 *spoken, local*: a north-easterly wind

His only eccentricity, to which he would cheerfully admit if you asked him, was talking aloud to himself when he was alone. This habit, he said, grew from the fact that the kind of work he did left him entirely by himself for ten hours a day, six days a week. 'It keeps me company,' he said, 'hearing me own voice now and again.'

He biked on down the road, pedaling hard against the brutal wind.

'All right,' he said, 'all right, why don't you blow a bit? Is that the best you can do? My goodness me, I hardly know you're there this morning!' The wind howled around him and snapped at his coat and squeezed its way through the pores of the heavy wool, through his jacket underneath, through his shirt and vest, and it touched his bare skin with an icy fingertip. 'Why,' he said, 'it's **lukewarm** you are today. You'll have to do a sight[7] better than that if you're going to make me shiver.'

And now the darkness was diluting into a pale gray morning light, and Gordon Butcher could see the cloudy roof of the sky very low above his head and flying with the wind. Gray blue the clouds were, **flecked** here and there with black, a solid mass from horizon to horizon, the whole thing moving with the wind, sliding past above his head like a great gray sheet of metal unrolling. All around him lay the bleak and lonely fen country of Suffolk, mile upon mile of it that went on for ever.

He pedaled on. He rode through the outskirts of the little town of Mildenhall and headed for the village of West Row, where the man called Ford had his place.

He had left his tractor at Ford's the day before because his next job was to plow up four and a half acres[8] on Thistley Green for Ford. It was not Ford's land; it is important to remember this. But Ford was the one who had asked him to do the work.

Actually a farmer called Rolfe owned the four and a half acres.

Rolfe had asked Ford to get it plowed because Ford, like Gordon Butcher, did plowing jobs for other men. The difference

7 *impolite*: usually '*a damn sight better/bigger/more*' etc, used to emphasize something strongly
8 a unit for measuring the surface area of land, equal to 4,047 square metres

between Ford and Gordon Butcher was that Ford was somewhat grander. He was a fairly **prosperous** small-time agricultural engineer who had a nice house and a large yard full of sheds filled with farm implements and machinery. Gordon Butcher had only his one tractor.

On this occasion, however, when Rolfe had asked Ford to plow up his four and a half acres on Thistley Green, Ford was too busy to do the work so he hired Gordon Butcher to do it for him.

There was no one about in Ford's yard when Butcher rode in. He parked his bike, filled up his tractor with paraffin and gasoline, warmed the engine, hitched the plow behind, mounted the high seat and drove out to Thistley Green.

The field was not half a mile away, and around eight-thirty Butcher drove the tractor in through the gate onto the field itself. Thistley Green was maybe a hundred acres all told, with a low hedge running round it. And although it was actually one large field, different parts of it were owned by different men. These separate parts were easy to define because each was cultivated in its own way. Rolfe's plot of four and a half acres was over to one side near the southern boundary fence. Butcher knew where it was and drove his tractor round the edge of the field, then inward until he was on the plot.

The plot was barley **stubble** now, covered with the short and rotting yellow stalks of barley harvested last fall, and only recently it had been broad-sheared[9] so that now it was ready for the plow.

'Deep-plow it,' Ford had said to Butcher the day before. 'It's for sugar beet. Rolfe's putting sugar beet in there.'

They only plow about four inches[10] down for barley, but for sugar beet they plow deep, to ten or twelve inches. A horse-drawn plow can't plow as deep as that. It was only since tractors came along that the farmers had been able to deep-plow properly. Rolfe's land had been deep-plowed for sugar beet some years

9 *agricultural*: cut shorter
10 a unit for measuring length. An inch is equal to 2.54 centimetres. There are 12 inches in one foot.

before this, but it wasn't Butcher who had done the plowing and no doubt the job had been **skimped** a bit and the plowman had not gone quite as deep as he should. Had he done so, what was about to happen today would probably have happened then, and that would have been a different story.

Gordon Butcher began to plow. Up and down the field he went, lowering the plow deeper and deeper each trip until at last it was cutting twelve inches into the ground and turning up a smooth, even wave of black earth as it went.

The wind was coming faster now, rushing in from the killer sea, sweeping over the flat Norfolk fields, past Saxthorpe and Reepham and Honingham and Swaffham and Larling and over the border to Suffolk, to Mildenhall and to Thistley Green where Gordon Butcher sat upright high on the seat of his tractor, driving back and forth over the plot of yellow barley stubble that belonged to Rolfe. Gordon Butcher could smell the sharp crisp smell of snow not far away; he could see the low roof of the sky, no longer flecked with black, but pale and whitish gray sliding by overhead like a solid sheet of metal unrolling.

'Well,' he said, raising his voice above the clatter of the tractor, 'you are surely angry at somebody today. What an almighty[11] fuss it is now of blowin' and whistlin' and freezin'. Like a woman,' he added. 'Just like a woman does sometimes in the evening.' And he kept his eye upon the line of the furrow[12], and he smiled.

At noon he stopped the tractor, dismounted and fished in his pocket for his lunch. He found it and sat on the ground in the lee of one of the huge tractor wheels. He ate large pieces of bread and very small pieces of cheese. He had nothing to drink, for his only Thermos[13] had got smashed by the **jolting** of the tractor two weeks before, and in wartime, for this was in January 1942, you could not buy another anywhere. For about fifteen minutes he sat on the ground in the shelter of the wheel and ate his lunch. Then he got up and examined his peg.

11 *informal*: used for emphasizing how great, loud, or serious something is
12 a line that a farmer digs in the soil with a plough where a crop will be planted
13 *trademark, Thermos flask*: a container that keeps liquids hot or cold

Unlike many plowmen, Butcher always hitched his plow to the tractor with a wooden peg so that if the plow fouled a root or a large stone, the peg would simply break at once, leaving the plow behind and saving the plowshares from serious damage. All over the black fen country, just below the surface, lie enormous trunks of ancient oak trees, and a wooden peg will save a plowshare many times a week out there. Although Thistley Green was well-cultivated land – field land, not fen land – Butcher was taking no chances with his plow.

He examined the wooden peg, found it **sound**, mounted the tractor again and went on with his plowing.

The tractor nosed back and forth over the ground, leaving a smooth brown wave of soil behind it. And still the wind blew colder, but it did not snow.

Around three o'clock the thing happened.

There was a slight jolt, the wooden peg broke, and the tractor left the plow behind. Butcher stopped, dismounted and walked back to the plow to see what it had struck. It was surprising for this to have happened here, on field land. There should be no oak trees underneath the soil in this place.

He **knelt down** beside the plow and began to scoop the soil away around the point of the plowshare. The lower tip of the share was twelve inches down. There was a lot of soil to be scooped up. He dug his gloved fingers into the earth and scooped it out with both hands. Six inches down . . . eight inches . . . ten inches . . . twelve. He slid his fingers along the blade of the plowshare until they reached the forward point of it. The soil was loose and **crumbly**, and it kept falling back into the hole he was digging. He could not therefore see the twelve-inch-deep point of the share. He could only feel it. And now he could feel that the point was indeed **lodged** against something solid. He scooped away more earth. He enlarged the hole. It was necessary to see clearly what sort of an obstacle he had struck. If it was fairly small, then perhaps he could dig it out with his hands and get on with the job. If it was a tree trunk, he would have to go back to Ford's and fetch a **spade**.

'Come on,' he said aloud. 'I'll have you out of there, you hidden demon, you rotten old thing.' And suddenly, as the gloved fingers scraped away a final handful of black earth, he caught sight of the curved **rim** of something flat, like the rim of a huge thick plate, sticking up out of the soil. He rubbed the rim with his fingers, and he rubbed again. Then all at once, the rim gave off a greenish **glint**, and Gordon Butcher bent his head closer and closer still, peering down into the little hole he had dug with his hands. For one last time, he rubbed the rim clean with his fingers, and in a flash of light, he saw clearly the unmistakable blue-green **crust** of ancient buried metal, and his heart stood still.

It should be explained here that farmers in this part of Suffolk, and particularly in the Mildenhall area, have for years been turning up ancient objects from the soil. Flint arrowheads from very long ago have been found in considerable numbers, but more interesting than that, Roman pottery and Roman implements have also been found. It is known that the Romans favored this part of the country during their occupation of Britain, and all local farmers are therefore well aware of the possibility of finding something interesting during a day's work. And so there was a kind of permanent awareness among Mildenhall people of the presence of treasure underneath the earth of their land.

Gordon Butcher's reaction, as soon as he saw the rim of that enormous plate, was a curious one. He immediately drew away. Then he got to his feet and turned his back on what he had just seen. He paused only long enough to switch off the engine of his tractor before he walked off fast in the direction of the road.

He did not know precisely what impulse caused him to stop digging and walk away. He will tell you that the only thing he can remember about those first few seconds was the whiff[14] of danger that came to him from that little patch of greenish blue. The moment he touched it with his fingers, something electric went through his body, and there came to him a powerful **premonition** that this was a thing that could destroy the peace and happiness of many people.

14 *mainly literary*: a slight amount or sign of something

In the beginning, all he had wished was to be away from it, to leave it behind him and be done with it forever. But after he had gone a hundred yards[15] or so, he began to slow his pace. At the gate leading out from Thistley Green, he stopped.

'What in the world is the matter with you, Mr. Gordon Butcher?' he said aloud to the howling wind. 'Are you frightened or something? No, I'm not frightened. But I'll tell you straight, I'm not keen to handle this alone.'

That was when he thought of Ford.

He thought of Ford at first because it was for him that he was working. He thought of him second because he knew that Ford was a kind of collector of old **stuff**, of all the old stones and arrowheads that people kept digging up from time to time in the district, which they brought to Ford and which Ford placed upon the mantel[16] in his parlor. It was believed that Ford sold these things, but no one knew or cared how he did it.

Gordon Butcher turned toward Ford's place and walked fast out of the gate onto the narrow road, down the road around the sharp left-hand corner and so to the house. He found Ford in his large shed bending over a damaged harrow[17], mending it. Butcher stood by the door and said, 'Mr. Ford !'

Ford looked around without straightening his body.

'Well, Gordon,' he said, 'what is it?'

Ford was middle-aged or a little older, bald-headed, long-nosed, with a clever foxy look about his face. His mouth was thin and **sour**, and when he looked at you, and when you saw the tightness of his mouth and the thin sour line of his lips, you knew that this was a mouth that never smiled. His chin receded, his nose was long and sharp and he had the air about him of a sour old crafty fox from the woods.

'What is it?' he said, looking up from the harrow.

Gordon Butcher stood by the door, blue-cheeked with cold, a little out of breath, rubbing his hands slowly one against the other.

15 a unit for measuring length. There are three feet or 36 inches in a yard. One yard is equal to 0.91 metres.

16 *mainly US, also spelt* 'mantle': a shelf above the opening of a fireplace

17 *agriculture*: a machine which a farmer pulls over ploughed land to break up the soil

'The tractor left the plow behind,' he said quietly. 'There's metal down there. I saw it.'

Ford's head gave a **jerk**. 'What kind of metal?' he said sharply.

'Flat. Quite flat like a sort of huge plate.'

'You didn't dig it out?' Ford had straightened up now and there was a glint of eagles in his eyes.

Butcher said, 'No, I left it alone and came straight on here.'

Ford walked quickly over to the corner and took his coat off the nail. He found a cap and gloves, then he found a spade and went toward the door. There was something odd, he noticed, in Butcher's manner.

'You're sure it was metal?'

'Crusted up,' Butcher said. 'But it was metal all right.'

'How deep?'

'Twelve inches down. At least the top of it was twelve inches down. The rest is deeper.'

'How d'you know it was a plate?'

'I don't,' Butcher said. 'I only saw a little bit of the rim, but it looked like a plate to me. An enormous plate.'

Ford's foxy face went quite white with excitement. 'Come on,' he said. 'We'll go back and see.'

The two men walked out of the shed into the fierce, ever-mounting fury of the wind. Ford shivered.

'Curse this filthy weather,' he said. 'Curse and blast[18] this filthy freezing weather,' and he sank his pointed foxy face deep into the collar of his coat and began to ponder[19] upon the possibilities of Butcher's find.

One thing Ford knew that Butcher did not know. He knew that back in 1932 a man called Lethbridge, a lecturer in Anglo-Saxon antiquities at Cambridge University, had been excavating in the district and that he had actually unearthed the foundations of a Roman villa on Thistley Green itself. Ford was not forgetting that, and he quickened his pace. Butcher walked beside him without speaking, and soon they were there. They

18 *spoken:* 'curse' and 'blast' are both used for showing that you are angry
19 *formal:* to think carefully about something for a long time before reaching a decision

went through the gate and over the field to the plow, which lay about ten yards behind the tractor.

Ford knelt down beside the front of the plow and peered into the small hole Gordon Butcher had dug with his hands. He touched the rim of green-blue metal with a gloved finger. He scraped away a bit more earth. He leaned farther forward so that his pointed nose was right down the hole. He ran his fingers over the rough green surface. Then he stood up and said, 'Let's get the plow out of the way and do some digging.' Although there were fireworks exploding in his head and shivers running all over his body, Ford kept his voice very soft and casual.

Between them they pulled the plow back a couple of yards.

'Give me the spade,' Ford said, and he began cautiously to dig the soil away in a circle about three feet in diameter around the exposed patch of metal. When the hole was two feet deep, he threw away the spade and used his hands. He knelt down and scraped the soil away, and gradually the little patch of metal grew and grew until at last there lay exposed before them the great round disk of an enormous plate. It was fully twenty-four inches in diameter. The lower point of the plow had just caught the raised center rim of the plate, for one could see the dent.

Carefully Ford lifted it out of the hole. He got to his feet and stood wiping the soil away from it, turning it over and over in his hands. There was nothing much to see, for the whole surface was crusted over with a thick layer of a hard greenish-blue substance. But he knew that it was an enormous plate or dish of great weight and thickness. It weighed about eighteen pounds[20]!

Ford stood in the field of yellow barley stubble and gazed at the huge plate. His hands began to shake. A tremendous and almost unbearable excitement started boiling up inside him, and it was not easy for him to hide it. But he did his best.

'Some sort of a dish,' he said.

Butcher was kneeling on the ground beside the hole. 'Must be pretty old,' he said.

'Could be old,' Ford said. 'But it's all rusted up and eaten away.'

20 about 8 kg

'That doesn't look like **rust** to me,' Butcher said. 'That greenish stuff isn't rust. It's something else.'

'It's green rust,' Ford said rather superbly, and that ended the discussion.

Butcher, still on his knees, was poking about casually in the now three-foot-wide hole with his gloved hands. 'There's another one down here,' he said.

Instantly, Ford laid the great dish on the ground. He knelt beside Butcher, and within minutes they had unearthed a second large green-encrusted plate. This one was a shade smaller than the first, and deeper. More of a bowl than a dish.

Ford stood up and held the new find in his hands. Another heavy one. And now he knew for certain they were onto something absolutely tremendous. They were onto Roman treasure, and almost without question it was pure silver. Two things pointed to it being pure silver. First the weight, and second, the particular type of green crust caused by oxidation[21].

How often is a piece of Roman silver discovered in the world? Almost never anymore.

And have pieces as large as this ever been unearthed before? Ford wasn't sure, but he very much doubted it.

Worth millions it must be.

Worth literally millions of pounds.

His breath, coming fast, was making little white clouds in the freezing atmosphere.

'There's still more down here, Mr. Ford,' Butcher was saying. 'I can feel bits of it all over the place. You'll need the spade again.'

The third piece they got out was another large plate, somewhat similar to the first. Ford placed it in the barley stubble with the other two.

Then Butcher felt the first flake of snow upon his cheek, and he looked up and saw over to the northeast a great white curtain drawn across the sky, a solid wall of snow flying forward on the wings of the wind.

21 *scientific*: the process by which a substance combines with oxygen or loses hydrogen; in everyday speech, this is called 'rust'

'Here she comes!' he said, and Ford looked around and saw the snow moving down upon them and said, 'It's a blizzard. It's a filthy, stinking blizzard!'

The two men stared at the blizzard as it raced across the fens toward them. Then it was on them, and all around was snow and snowflakes, white wind with snowflakes slanting in the wind and snowflakes in the eyes and ears and mouth and down the neck and all around. And when Butcher glanced down at the ground a few seconds later it was already white.

'That's all we want,' Ford said. 'A filthy, rotten, stinking blizzard,' and he shivered and sunk his sharp and foxy face deeper into the collar of his coat. 'Come on,' he said. 'See if there's any more.'

Butcher knelt down again and poked around in the soil, then in the slow and casual manner of a man having a lucky dip[22] in a barrel of sawdust, he pulled out another plate and held it out to Ford, who took it and put it down beside the rest. Now Ford knelt down beside Butcher and began to dip into the soil with him.

For a whole hour the two men stayed out there digging and scratching in that three-foot patch of soil. And during that hour they found and laid upon the ground beside them no less than thirty-three separate pieces! There were dishes, bowls, goblets, spoons, ladles and several other things, all of them crusted over but each one recognizable for what it was. And all the while the blizzard swirled around them and the snow gathered in little mounds on their caps and on their shoulders and the flakes melted on their faces so that rivers of icy water trickled down their necks. A large globule of half-frozen liquid dangled continually, like a snowdrop, from the end of Ford's pointed nose.

They worked in silence. It was too cold to speak. And as one precious article after the other was unearthed, Ford laid them carefully on the ground in rows, pausing every now and then to

22 a game in which you put your hand into a box that contains a lot of small prizes and choose one without looking

wipe the snow away from a dish or a spoon that was in danger of being completely covered.

At last Ford said, 'That's the lot, I think.'

'Yes.'

Ford stood up and stamped his feet on the ground. 'Got a **sack** in the tractor?' he said, and while Butcher walked over to fetch the sack, he turned and gazed upon the three-and-thirty[23] pieces lying in the snow at his feet. He counted them again. If they were silver, which they surely must be, and if they were Roman, which they undoubtedly were, then this was a discovery that would rock the world.

Butcher called to him from the tractor, 'It's only a dirty old sack.'

'It'll do.'

Butcher brought the sack over and held it open while Ford carefully put the articles into it. They all went in except one. The massive two-foot plate was too large for the neck of the sack.

The two men were really cold now. For over an hour they had knelt and scratched about out there in the open field with the blizzard swirling around them. Already, nearly six inches of snow had fallen. Butcher was half frozen. His cheeks were dead white, blotched with blue; his feet were numb like wood, and when he moved his legs he could not feel the ground beneath him. He was much colder than Ford. Butcher's coat and clothes were not so thick, and ever since early morning he had been sitting high up on the seat of the tractor, exposed to the bitter wind. His blue-white face was tight and unmoving. All he wanted was to get home to his family and to the fire that he knew would be burning in the grate.

Ford, on the other hand, was not thinking about the cold. His mind was concentrated solely upon one thing – how to get possession of this fabulous treasure. His position, as he knew very well, was not a strong one.

In England there is a very curious law about finding any kind of gold or silver treasure. This law goes back hundreds of years

23 *old-fashioned*: thirty-three

and is still strictly enforced today. The law states that if a person digs up out of the ground, even out of his own garden, a piece of metal that is either *gold* or *silver*, it automatically becomes what is known as treasure trove and is the property of the Crown. The Crown doesn't in these days mean the actual king or queen. It means the country or the government. The law also states that it is a criminal offence to **conceal** such a find. You are simply not allowed to hide the stuff and keep it for yourself. You must report it at once, preferably to the police. And if you do report it at once, you as the finder will be entitled to receive from the government in money the full amount of the market value of the article. You are not required to report the digging up of other metals. You are allowed to find as much valuable pewter, bronze, copper or even platinum as you wish, and you can keep it all; but not gold or silver.

The other curious part of this curious law is this: it is the person who *discovers* the treasure in the first place who gets the reward from the government. The owner of the land gets nothing – unless, of course, the finder is trespassing[24] on the land when he makes the discovery. But if the finder of the treasure has been hired by the owner to do a job on his land, then he, the finder, gets all the reward.

In this case, the finder was Gordon Butcher. Furthermore, he was not trespassing. He was performing a job that he had been hired to do. This treasure therefore belonged to Butcher and to no one else. All he had to do was take it and show it to an expert who would immediately identify it as silver, then turn it in to the police. In time, he would receive from the government 100 percent of its value – perhaps a million pounds sterling.

All this left Ford out in the cold[25], and Ford knew it. He had no rights whatsoever to the treasure by law. Thus, as he must have told himself at the time, his only chance of getting hold of the stuff for himself lay in the fact that Butcher was an ignorant man who didn't know the law and who did not anyway have the

24 to go into a place without the owner's permission
25 'leave someone out in the cold': to deliberately not include someone in an activity or group

faintest idea of the value of the find. The probability was that in a few days Butcher would forget all about it. He was too simple-minded a fellow, too artless, too trusting, too unselfish to give the matter much thought.

Now, out there in the desolate snow-swept field, Ford bent down and took hold of the huge dish with one hand. He raised it but he did not lift it. The lower rim remained resting in the snow. With his other hand, he grasped the top of the sack. He didn't lift that either. He just held it. And there he **stooped** amid the swirling snowflakes, both hands embracing, as it were, the treasure, but not actually taking it. It was a subtle and a canny gesture. It managed somehow to signify ownership before ownership had been discussed. A child plays the same game when he reaches out and closes his fingers over the biggest chocolate éclair on the plate and then says, 'Can I have this one, Mummy?' He's already got it.

'Well, Gordon,' Ford said, stooping over, holding the sack and the great dish in his gloved fingers. 'I don't suppose you want any of this old stuff.'

It was not a question. It was a statement of fact framed as a question.

The blizzard was still raging. The snow was falling so densely, the two men could hardly see one another.

'You ought to get along home and warm yourself up,' Ford went on. 'You look frozen to death.'

'I feel frozen to death,' Butcher said.

'Then you get on that tractor quick and hurry home,' said the thoughtful, kindhearted Ford. 'Leave the plow here and leave your bike at my place. The important thing is to get back and warm yourself up before you catch pneumonia.'

'I think that's just what I will do, Mr. Ford,' Butcher said. 'Can you manage all right with that sack? It's mighty heavy.'

'I might not even bother about it today,' Ford said casually. 'I just might leave it here and come back for it another time. Rusty old stuff.'

'So long then, Mr. Ford.'

'Bye, Gordon.'

Gordon Butcher mounted the tractor and drove away into the blizzard.

Ford hoisted the sack onto his shoulder, and then, not without difficulty he lifted the massive dish with his other hand and tucked it under his arm.

I am carrying, he told himself, as he trudged through the snow, I am now carrying what is probably the biggest treasure ever dug up in the whole history of England.

When Gordon Butcher came stamping and blowing through the back door of his small brick house late that afternoon, his wife was ironing by the fire. She looked up and saw his blue-white face and snow-encrusted clothes.

'My goodness, Gordon, you look froze to death!' she cried.

'I am,' he said. 'Help me off with these clothes, love. My fingers aren't hardly working at all.'

She took off his gloves, his coat, his jacket, his wet shirt. She pulled off his boots and socks. She fetched a towel and rubbed his chest and shoulders vigorously all over to restore the circulation. She rubbed his feet.

'Sit down there by the fire,' she said, 'and I'll get you a hot cup of tea.'

Later, when he was settled comfortably in the warmth with dry clothes on his back and the mug of tea in his hand, he told her what had happened that afternoon.

'He's a foxy one, that Mr. Ford,' she said, not looking up from her ironing. 'I never did like him.'

'He got pretty excited about it all, I can tell you that,' Gordon Butcher said. '**Jumpy** as a jackrabbit he was.'

'That may be,' she said. 'But you ought to have had more sense than to go crawling about on your hands and knees in a freezing blizzard just because Mr. Ford said to do it.'

'I'm all right,' Gordon Butcher said. 'I'm warming up nicely now.'

And that, believe it or not, was about the last time the subject of the treasure was discussed in the Butcher household for some years.

The reader should be reminded here that this was wartime, 1942. Britain was totally absorbed in the desperate war against Hitler and Mussolini. Germany was bombing England, and England was bombing Germany, and nearly every night Gordon Butcher heard the roar of engines from the big airbase at nearby Mildenhall as the bombers took off for Hamburg, Berlin, Kiel, Wilhelmshaven or Frankfurt. Sometimes he would wake in the early hours and hear them coming home, and sometimes the Germans flew over to bomb the base, and the Butcher house would shake with the crumph[26] and crash of bombs not far away.

Butcher himself was exempt[27] from military service. He was a farmer, a skilled plowman, and they had told him when he volunteered for the army in 1939 that he was not wanted. The island's food supplies must be kept going, they said, and it was **vital** that men like him stay on their jobs and cultivate the land.

Ford, being in the same business, was also exempt. He was a bachelor, living alone, and he was thus able to live a secret life and do secret things within the walls of his home.

And so, on that terrible snowy afternoon when they dug up the treasure, Ford carried it home and laid everything out on a table in the back room.

Thirty-three separate pieces! They covered the entire table. And by the look of it, they were in marvelous condition. Silver does not rust. The green crust of oxidation can even be a protection for the surface of the metal underneath. And with care, it could all be removed.

Ford decided to use an ordinary domestic silver polish known as Silvo, and he bought a large stock of it from the ironmonger's[28] shop in Mildenhall. He took first the great two-foot plate, which weighed more than eighteen pounds. He worked on it in the evenings. He soaked it all over with Silvo. He rubbed and rubbed. He worked patiently on this single dish every night for more than sixteen weeks.

26 possibly an invented word (Dahl invented many words in his books for children); here, possibly the low sound of a heavy object hitting the ground and collapsing
27 *formal*: allowed to ignore something such as a rule, obligation, or payment
28 *old-fashioned British*: a shop that sells tools and other metal goods

At last, one memorable evening, there showed beneath his rubbing a small area of shining silver, and on the silver, raised up and beautifully worked, there was a part of a man's head.

He kept at it, and gradually the little patch of shining metal spread and spread, the blue-green crust crept outward to the edges of the plate until finally the top surface of the great dish lay before him in its full glory, covered all over with a wondrous[29] pattern of animals and men and many odd legendary things.

Ford was astounded by the beauty of the great plate. It was filled with life and movement. There was a fierce face with tangled hair, a dancing goat with a human head, there were men and women and animals of many kinds cavorting around the rim, and no doubt all of them told a story.

Next he set about cleaning the reverse side of the plate. Weeks and weeks it took. And when the work was completed and the whole plate on both sides was shining like a star, he placed it safely in the lower cupboard of his big oak sideboard and locked the cupboard door.

One by one, he tackled the remaining thirty-two pieces. A **mania** had taken hold of him now, a fierce compulsion to make every item shine in all its silver brilliance. He wanted to see all thirty-three pieces laid out on the big table in a dazzling **array** of silver. He wanted that more than anything else, and he worked desperately hard to achieve his wish.

He cleaned the two smaller dishes next, then the large fluted bowl, then the five long-handled ladles, the goblets, the wine cups, the spoons. Every single piece was cleaned with equal care and made to shine with equal brilliance; and when they were all done two years had passed, and it was 1944.

But no strangers were allowed to look. Ford discussed the matter with no man or woman, and Rolfe, the owner of the plot on Thistley Green where the treasure had been found, knew nothing except that Ford, or someone Ford had hired, had plowed his land extremely well and very deep.

One can guess why Ford hid the treasure instead of reporting it to the police as treasure trove. Had he reported it, it would

29 *literary*: impressive and beautiful or exciting

have been taken away and Gordon Butcher would have been rewarded as the finder. Rewarded with a fortune. So the only thing Ford could do was to **hang on to** it and hide it in the hope, presumably, of selling it quietly to some dealer or collector at a later date.

It is possible, of course, to take a more charitable view and assume that Ford kept the treasure solely because he loved beautiful things and wanted to have them around him. No one will ever know the true answer.

Another year went by.

The war against Hitler was won.

And then, in 1946, just after Easter, there was a knock on the door of Ford's house. Ford opened it.

'Why hello, Mr. Ford. How are you after all these years?'

'Hello, Dr Fawcett,' Ford said. 'You been keeping all right?'

'I'm fine, thank you,' Dr Fawcett said. 'It's been a long time, hasn't it?'

'Yes,' Ford said. 'That old war kept us all pretty busy.'

'May I come in?' Dr Fawcett asked.

'Of course,' Ford said. 'Come on in.'

Dr Hugh Alderson Fawcett was a keen and learned archaeologist who before the war had made a point of visiting Ford once a year in search of old stones or arrowheads. Ford had usually collected a batch of such items during the twelve months and he was always willing to sell them to Fawcett. They were seldom of great value, but now and again something quite good had turned up.

'Well,' said Fawcett, taking off his coat in the little hall, 'Well, well, well. It's been nearly seven years since I was here last.'

'Yes, it's been a long time,' Ford said.

Ford led him into the front room and showed him a box of flint arrowheads that had been picked up in the district. Some were good, others not so good. Fawcett picked through them, sorted them, and a deal was made.

'Nothing else?'

'No, I don't think so.'

Ford wished fervently that Dr Fawcett had never come. He wished even more fervently that he would go away.

It was at this point that Ford noticed something that made him sweat. He saw suddenly that he had left lying on the mantle over the fireplace the two most beautiful of the Roman spoons from the treasure hoard. These spoons had fascinated him because each was inscribed with the name of a Roman girl child. One was Pascentia, the other was Pappitedo. Rather lovely names.

Ford, sweating with fear, tried to place himself between Dr Fawcett and the mantlepiece. He might even, he thought, be able to slip the spoons into his pocket if he got the chance.

He didn't get the chance.

Perhaps Ford had polished them so well that a little flash of reflected light from the silver caught the doctor's eye. Who knows? The fact remains that Fawcett saw them. The moment he saw them, he **pounced** like a tiger.

'Great heavens alive[30]!' he cried. 'What are these?'

'Pewter,' Ford said, sweating more than ever. 'Just a couple of old pewter spoons.'

'Pewter?' cried Fawcett, turning one of the spoons over in his fingers. 'Pewter! You call this pewter?'

'That's right,' Ford said. 'It's pewter.'

'You know what this is?', Fawcett said, his voice going high with excitement. 'Shall I tell you what this really is?'

'You don't have to tell me' Ford said, truculent[31]. 'I know what it is. It's old pewter. And quite nice, too.'

Fawcett was reading the inscription in Roman letters on the scoop of the spoon. 'Pappitedo!' he cried.

'What's that mean?' Ford asked him.

Fawcett picked up the other spoon. 'Pascentia,' he said. 'Beautiful! These are the names of Roman children! And these spoons, my friend, are made of solid silver! Solid Roman silver!'

'Not possible,' Ford said.

---

30 *exclamation, old-fashioned:* sometimes just *'Heavens!'* used for showing that you are very surprised

31 *formal:* easily annoyed and always ready to argue or fight

'They're magnificent!' Fawcett cried out, going into raptures[32]. 'They're perfect! They're unbelievable! Where on earth did you find them? It's most important to know where you found them! Was there anything else?' Fawcett was hopping about all over the room.

'Well . . .' Ford said, licking dry lips.

'You must report them at once!' Fawcett cried. 'They're treasure trove! The British Museum is going to want these and that's for certain! How long have you had them?'

'Just a little while,' Ford told him.

'And *who* found them?' Fawcett asked, looking straight at him. 'Did you find them yourself or did you get them from somebody else? This is vital! The finder will be able to tell us all about it!'

Ford felt the walls of the room closing in on him and he didn't quite know what to do.

'Come on, man! Surely you know where you got them! Every detail will have to come out when you hand them in. Promise me you'll go to the police with them at once!'

'Well . . .' Ford said.

'If you don't, then I'm afraid I shall be forced to report it myself,' Fawcett told him. 'It's my duty.'

The **game was up** now, and Ford knew it. A thousand questions would be asked. How did you find it? When did you find it? What were you doing? Where was the exact spot? Whose land were you plowing? And sooner or later, inevitably, the name of Gordon Butcher would have to come into it. It was unavoidable. And then, when Butcher was questioned, he would remember the size of the hoard and tell them all about it.

So the game was up. And the only thing to do at this point was to unlock the doors of the big **sideboard** and show the entire hoard to Dr Fawcett.

Ford's excuse for keeping it all and not turning it in would have to be that he thought it was pewter. So long as he stuck to that, he told himself, they couldn't do anything to him.

Dr Fawcett would probably have a heart attack when he saw what there was in that cupboard.

32 *phrase, 'go into raptures'*: go into an extremely happy and excited state

'There is actually quite a bit more of it,' Ford said.

'Where?' cried Fawcett, spinning round. 'Where, man, where? Lead me to it!'

'I really thought it was pewter,' Ford said, moving slowly and very reluctantly forward to the oak sideboard. 'Otherwise, I would naturally have reported it at once.'

He bent down and unlocked the lower doors of the sideboard. He opened the doors.

And then Dr Hugh Alderson Fawcett very nearly did have a heart attack. He flung himself on his knees. He gasped. He choked. He began **spluttering** like an old kettle. He reached out for the great silver dish. He took it. He held it in shaking hands and his face went as white as snow. He didn't speak. He couldn't. He was literally – physically and mentally – struck absolutely dumb[33] by the sight of the treasure.

The interesting part of the story ends here. The rest is routine. Ford went to Mildenhall police station and made a report. The police came at once and collected all thirty-three pieces, and they were sent under guard to the British Museum for examination.

Then an urgent message from the museum to the Mildenhall police. It was **far and away** the finest Roman silver ever found in the British Isles. It was of enormous value. The museum (which is really a public governmental institution) wished to acquire it. In fact, they insisted upon acquiring it.

The wheels of the law began to turn. An official inquest and hearing was arranged at the nearest large town, Bury St Edmunds. The silver was moved there under special police guard. Ford was summoned to appear before the coroner and a jury of fourteen, while Gordon Butcher, that good and quiet man, was ordered also to present himself to give evidence.

On Monday, July 1, 1946, the hearing took place, and the coroner cross-questioned Ford closely.

'You thought it was pewter?'

'Yes.'

33 *phrase, mainly literary*, 'to be struck dumb': temporarily unable or unwilling to speak, especially because you are very shocked

'Even after you had cleaned it?'

'Yes,'

'You took no steps to inform any experts of the find?'

'No.'

'What did you intend to do with the articles?'

'Nothing. Just keep them.'

And when he had concluded his evidence, Ford asked permission to go outside into the fresh air because he said he felt faint. Nobody was surprised.

Then Butcher was called, and in a few simple words he told of his part in the affair.

Dr Fawcett gave his evidence, as did several other learned archaeologists, all of whom **testified** to the extreme rarity of the treasure. They said that it was of the fourth century after Christ; that it was the table silver of a wealthy Roman family; that it had probably been buried by the owner's bailiff[34] to save it from the Picts and Scots, who swept down from the north in about AD 365 and laid waste[35] many Roman settlements. The man who buried it had probably been **liquidated** either by a Pict or a Scot, and the treasure had remained concealed a foot below the soil ever since. The workmanship, said the experts, was magnificent. Some of it may have been executed in England, but more probably the articles were made in Italy or in Egypt. The great plate was of course the finest piece. The head in the center was that of Neptune, the sea god, with dolphins in his hair and seaweed in his beard. All around him, sea nymphs and sea monsters gamboled. On the broad rim of the plate stood Bacchus and his attendants. There was wine and revelry. Hercules was there, quite drunk, supported by two satyrs, his lion's skin fallen from his shoulders. Pan was there too, dancing upon his goat-legs with his pipes in his hand. And everywhere there were Maenads, female devotees of Bacchus, rather **tipsy** women.

The court was told also that several of the spoons bore the monogram[36] of Christ (*Chi-Rho*) and that the two that

34 someone whose job is to look after a farm or land that belongs to someone else

35 *phrase, 'to lay waste'*: to cause very serious damage to a place, especially in a war

36 a design using the first letter of each of someone's names, usually sewn onto clothing or decorating an object

were inscribed with the names Pascentia and Pappitedo were undoubtedly christening presents.

The experts concluded their evidence, and the court **adjourned**. Soon the jury returned, and their verdict was astonishing. No blame was attached to anyone for anything, although the finder of the treasure was no longer entitled to receive full compensation from the Crown because the find had not been declared at once. Nevertheless, there would probably be a measure of compensation paid, and with this in view, the finders were declared to be jointly Ford and Butcher.

Not Butcher. Ford and Butcher.

There is no more to tell other than that the treasure was acquired by the British Museum, where it now stands proudly displayed in a large glass case for all to see. And already people have traveled great distances to go and look upon those lovely things that Gordon Butcher found beneath his plow on that cold and windy winter afternoon. One day, a book or two will be compiled about them, full of suppositions and abstruse[37] conclusions, and men who move in archaeological circles will talk forever about the Treasure of Mildenhall.

As a gesture, the museum rewarded the co-finders with one thousand pounds each. Butcher, the true finder, was happy and surprised to receive so much money. He did not realize that, had he been allowed to take the treasure home originally, he would almost certainly have revealed its existence and would thus have become eligible to receive 100 percent of its value, which could have been anything between half a million and a million pounds.

Nobody knows what Ford thought about it all. He must have been relieved and perhaps somewhat surprised when he heard that the court had believed his story about pewter.

But above all, he must have been **shattered** by the loss of his great treasure. For the rest of his life he would be **kicking himself** for leaving those two spoons on the mantle above the fireplace for Dr Fawcett to see.

37 *formal*: abstruse ideas or arguments are hard to understand, and are more complicated than necessary

Post-reading activities

Understanding the story

Use these questions to help you check that you have understood the story.

A note about the story

1 How did Roald Dahl know about the discovery of the treasure?
2 Why did Dahl decide to investigate?
3 Why did Butcher not want to speak to Dahl at first?
4 Do you think Ford refused to speak to Dahl for the same reason?

Butcher goes to work

5 What is Butcher's journey to work like?
6 What is Butcher's embarrassing habit? Is he ashamed of it? Why does he do it?
7 Why had Ford asked Butcher to do this work?
8 Does Butcher have to plough the whole field?
9 How do we know that he is a good ploughman? Why is this important?
10 What does he do to protect his machinery?
11 What is his reaction to seeing the buried object?
12 Why did he want Ford to help?
13 What is the first sign that Ford is interested in Butcher's discovery?

Butcher and Ford unearth the treasure

14 Why does Ford try not to show his excitement?
15 How many pieces of the treasure do they unearth before it starts to snow?
16 How many objects do they unearth in total?
17 Why is Butcher colder than Ford?
18 What is treasure trove?
19 How does Ford manipulate the situation so that he can take the treasure away?

At Ford's house

20 Why are Butcher and Ford not fighting in the war?
21 How long does it take Ford to clean the treasure? Why does he do it?
22 How do Ford and Dr Fawcett know each other?
23 Why does Ford suddenly become worried? What does he do then?
24 What is Fawcett's reaction to the spoons?
25 Why does Ford decide to show the rest of the hoard?
26 What did Fawcett say when he saw the rest of the hoard?

27 What was the objective of the inquest?

28 What defence does Ford decide to use as his reason for not telling anyone about the find?

29 What do the experts say was the probable reason that the treasure was buried?

30 What was Butcher's compensation? Is this what it should have been?

31 Which of these adjectives describe how Ford was probably feeling, according to Dahl:

a) upset   e) excited
b) angry with himself   f) unlucky
c) guilty   g) foolish
d) lucky

Language study

Grammar

Inversion in third conditional sentences

Form

Conditional sentences that describe the past are usually formed using *if* + past perfect / *would have* + past participle.

> **If** Butcher **had**n't **been** such a good ploughman, he probably **wouldn't have found** the treasure.

If can be omitted. Notice what happens to the verb.

> **Had** Butcher **not been** such a good ploughman, he probably wouldn't have found the treasure.

Notice how *had* and the subject, Butcher, swap places. Notice, too, the position of *not* before the past participle.

Use

The third conditional is used to speculate about the past. That is, to think about alternatives to what really happened. For that reason, it often expresses regrets that people have and is used to describe the consequences of actions that did not actually take place.

> *a) If I hadn't left those spoons on the mantelpiece, I'd have been able to keep the treasure for myself. (regret)*

b) If Ford had suggested to Butcher that they announce their discovery together, they might have been awarded a lot more money each. (possible consequence)

Notice in sentence b) the use of *might* rather than *would*. Other modals that can replace *would* include *could* and *should*.

The inverted structure makes the sentence sound more formal. It is more common in writing than speech. Compare sentence b) above with this one.

Had Ford **suggested** *to Butcher that they announce their discovery together, they might have been awarded a lot more money each.*

1 **Change the beginning of these sentences using *if* or inversion to make them less or more formal.**

1 If Butcher had been allowed to take the treasure home, he would almost certainly have revealed its existence.
2 If Dr Fawcett hadn't decided to visit Ford after the war, the treasure might have remained undiscovered.
3 Had Roald Dahl been unable to convince Butcher that he wasn't a reporter, the story might never have been written.
4 Had the wooden peg that connected Butcher's plough to the tractor been stronger, he might not have noticed there was anything buried there.

2 **Combine the two sentences to make a third sentence that speculates about the past. Use the inverted third conditional structure. Sometimes modal verbs other than *would* are appropriate.**

e.g. Ford knew about Roman artefacts. He was very interested in Butcher's discovery.

Had Ford not known about Roman artefacts, he might not have been very interested in Butcher's discovery.

1 Butcher didn't wear a warm coat. He got cold.
2 Butcher's wife wasn't interested in the treasure. She didn't tell people about her husband's discovery.
3 Butcher wasn't aware of the law of treasure trove. He didn't tell the authorities about what he had found.
4 The jury at the inquest were not suspicious of Ford. He was awarded £1,000.

Fronting in informal speech

Normal word order in English is *subject + verb + object/complement*, but we might change this order and put the object or complement first. This is called 'fronting'. We do it for different reasons. Firstly, it is one simple way to emphasize the object or complement. Also, it may be because when we speak the first thing that comes into our minds is the central information we want to express; we add the rest of the sentence afterwards.

> *Freezing I am!*

A writer may use fronting to imitate spoken English. Dahl sometimes uses fronting to mirror what Butcher or Ford are thinking.

> *Gray blue the clouds were. (Butcher on his way to work)*

> *Worth millions it must be. (Ford thinking about the treasure)*

3 Look at these examples from the story. What would the normal word order be?

   1 Why, lukewarm you are today.
   2 Around three o'clock the thing happened.
   3 One thing Ford knew that Butcher did not know.

4 Use fronting to change the word order of these sentences.

1 He was jumpy as a jackrabbit.
2 It took weeks and weeks.
3 He was much colder than Ford.

Vocabulary

Phrasal verbs with *up*

Look at the two sentences.

> *Fawcett **picked up** the other spoon.*

> *Ford showed him a box of flint arrowheads that he had **picked up** from local farmers.*

The verb *picked up* in the first sentence describes the upward movement of raising the spoon from the mantelpiece. In the second sentence the action is not the same. Here, *pick up* has a more general meaning of 'to get' or 'acquire'. There is no physical movement *up*. We can say that *pick up* in the first sentence has a literal meaning, whereas in the second sentence it has a figurative meaning.

Up has other meanings in phrasal verbs. Sometimes *up* has a meaning of doing something totally or completely.

He ate up all of the sandwiches.

Up also emphasizes the idea of increasing in a verb.

*The important thing is to **warm** yourself **up** before you catch pneumonia.*

Finally, *up* is used with verbs of travelling such as *go*. In the next sentence, remember that the fens, where the story takes place, have no hills, so *up* and *down* means *one way and the other way*.

***Up** and down the field he **went**, lowering the plow deeper and deeper.*

5 **Decide if the verbs in the following sentences have a literal meaning, or whether *up* has one of the meanings described above; travelling, increasing or doing something completely. Some may combine two meanings.**

a) *I **went up** to the British Museum in London.*

b) *He parked his bike and **filled up** his tractor with paraffin and gasoline.*

c) *There was a lot of soil to be **scooped up**.*

d) *Then he **stood up** and said, 'Let's get the plow out of the way and do some digging.'*

e) *He caught sight of the curved rim of something flat **sticking up** out of the soil.*

f) *A tremendous and almost unbearable excitement started **boiling up** inside him.*

g) *'But it's all **rusted up** and eaten away.'*

h) *He **looked up** and saw over to the northeast a great white curtain drawn across the sky*

6 **Complete the sentences below with the correct form of the verbs in the box and *up*.**

grow freeze look light pick speed go use jump drink

1 She .... from the newspaper when she heard her husband open the front door.

2 Where did you go yesterday? Oh, I .... to Harrington in the car.

3 By the end of the notebook all the ink in the pen had been
....

4 She took a torch which was powerful enough to .... the whole campsite.

5 'What do you want to be when you .... , Youssef?' 'Rich', the little boy replied.

6   'Will you stop telling me how to drive?! First you tell me to slow
    down and now you want me to .... !'
7   Finke .... and left the restaurant. He'd forgotten to pay
    the bill. He didn't get very far.
8   With just 3 weeks left before the wedding, Graham had still not
    .... the steps for his first dance with Jules, his fiancée.
    He was beginning to panic.
9   I was so frightened, I couldn't speak. I just ....
10 You need to train him not to .... A dog that big could
    hurt someone, you know.

Literary analysis

Plot

1   Number the events in the order in which they happened.

    [ ] Dahl went to Mildenhall.

    [ ] The war ended.

    [ ] Butcher drove to Thistley Green.

    [ ] Butcher stopped and ate lunch.

    [1] Ford asked Butcher to do a job for him.

    [ ] Butcher discovered something metallic in the ground.

    [ ] Butcher went to find Ford.

    [ ] Ford realized the value of the hoard.

    [ ] Butcher realized the value of the hoard.

    [ ] The treasure was moved under police guard to London.

    [ ] It started to snow.

    [ ] Ford carried the hoard home.

    [ ] Ford and Butcher were rewarded for finding the hoard.

    [ ] An inquest was held.

2   Look at the list again. Can you add any more key events?
3   What is the importance of the introductory 'Note about the next
    story' in the overall plot?
4   Which events in the story are accounts of what Dahl was told by
    Butcher? Which events would he have read about? Which events
    did he imagine?

5 Do you think that this story by Roald Dahl could be used as evidence by the Butcher family (Gordon died many years ago) to claim the full reward for the Mildenhall Treasure? Why/Why not?

6 What could Butcher have done to secure his reward for finding the treasure?

7 Does the story hold any moral message for you? If yes, what?

Character

8 Summarize the character of Butcher in one sentence.

9 Butcher has a curious reaction to seeing the plate in the ground and quickly goes to find Ford. What does this tell you about him?

10 Butcher recognizes Ford's excitement about the treasure but he doesn't think of asking him about it again. How can we explain this?

11 What sort of person is Mrs Butcher? Why do you think neither she nor Gordon Butcher talked about the treasure after that day?

12 Look at this extract. How does it help us feel sympathetic towards Butcher?

He was much colder than Ford. Butcher's coat and clothes were not so thick, and ever since early morning he had been sitting high up on the seat of the tractor, exposed to the bitter wind. His blue-white face was tight and unmoving. All he wanted was to get home to his family and to the fire that he knew would be burning in the grate.

13 In what other ways is Butcher portrayed as a good man?

14 How would you describe the relationship between Butcher and Ford?

Read the physical descriptions of the two men again.

He looked at you with steady blue eyes that were without any malice or cunning or greed. And the mouth didn't have those thin lines of bitterness around the edges that one so often sees on men who work the land and spend their days fighting the weather. (Butcher)

His mouth was thin and sour, and when he looked at you, and when you saw the tightness of his mouth and the thin sour line of his lips, you knew that this was a mouth that never smiled. His chin receded, his nose was long and sharp and he had the air about him of a sour old crafty fox from the woods. (Ford)

15 How does the first description – that of Butcher – prepare you for the later description of Ford?

16 When Ford suggests to Butcher that he should go home to warm up, why does Dahl call him 'thoughtful' and 'kindhearted'?

17 In what ways is Ford a typical villain? Draw up a list.

Narration

18 Dahl becomes a character in this story in the introduction when he talks about his visit to Mildenhall. What impression, if any, do you have of Dahl?

19 Dahl occasionally comments on the story he is telling, offering the reader some extra information or an opinion or reminding them of something. Here is an example:

   *His next job was to plow up four and a half acres on Thistley Green for Ford. It was not Ford's land; **it is important to remember this**. But Ford was the one who had asked him to do the work.*

   Find three more examples where Dahl comments directly on the story. What effect does this have on you as a reader?

20 Dahl describes the private thoughts and feelings of Ford in great detail even though he never interviewed Ford. Do you think Dahl is right to do this? Why/Why not?

21 Think about how the story would have been told differently if Dahl had interviewed Ford, and Butcher had refused to speak to Dahl. Think about what Ford knew, and what his attitude would have been to Butcher, to finding the treasure, and to his reasons for keeping it for himself.

Style

22 *The Mildenhall Treasure* was published in a collection of stories for young people who 'are no longer children and have not yet become adults'. What qualities, if any, does the story have that make it a story for young people?

23 Read these two extracts from early in the story. What words and phrases are repeated?

   And now the darkness was diluting into a pale gray morning light, and Gordon Butcher could see the cloudy roof of the sky very low above his head and flying with the wind. Gray blue the clouds were, flecked here and there with black, a solid mass from horizon to horizon, the whole thing moving with the wind, sliding past above his head like a great gray sheet of metal unrolling.

And a page later:

Gordon Butcher could smell the sharp crisp smell of snow not far away; he could see the low roof of the sky, no longer flecked with black, but pale and whitish gray sliding by overhead like a solid sheet of metal unrolling.

What is the effect of the repetition?

24 Look for repetition in the following parts of the story: when Butcher digs for the first time to see what has fouled the plough (Page 98); in the physical description of Ford (Page 100); in the account of Ford cleaning the silver (Page 109). What is the effect of this repetition?

25 Look at the length of the sentences and paragraphs in the following extract.

Ford stood up and held the new find in his hands. Another heavy one. And now he knew for certain they were onto something absolutely tremendous. They were onto Roman treasure, and almost without question it was pure silver. Two things pointed to it being pure silver. First the weight, and second, the particular type of green crust caused by oxidation.

How often is a piece of Roman silver discovered in the world?

Almost never anymore.

And have pieces as large as this ever been unearthed before?

Ford wasn't sure, but he very much doubted it.

Worth millions it must be.

Worth literally millions of pounds.

His breath, coming fast, was making little white clouds in the freezing atmosphere.

What is the effect of breaking the sentences up into paragraphs in this way? Can you find other examples of short, one line paragraphs in the text? Do they have the same effect or are they used for other reasons?

26 Dahl describes the reactions the characters have to the treasure in a dramatic way. In the following extracts, notice how the expressions describe a physical reaction to their excitement

*He saw clearly the ancient buried metal, and **his heart stood still**.*

*The moment he touched it with his fingers, **something electric went through his body**.*

*There were **fireworks exploding in his head** and **shivers running all over his body**.*

27 Can you find other examples of physical reactions like this?

Guidance to the above literary terms, answer keys to all the exercises and activities, plus a wealth of other reading-practice material, can be found at: <u>www.macmillanenglish.com/readers</u>.

The Yellow Wallpaper
by Charlotte Perkins Gilman

About the author

Charlotte Perkins Gilman was an American writer who is still well known today for her influence on the feminist movement. As well as fiction, she wrote essays and articles and toured the United States and Europe talking about women's roles in modern society. Her achievements would be impressive for anyone alive today; the fact that she was a woman living at the beginning of the 20th century makes her career all the more remarkable. What is also clear is that she had to make difficult personal sacrifices for her professional life and her beliefs.

Perkins' father left before she was born in 1860, which meant that the family was poor. She spent a lot of her childhood with aunts, one of whom was the famous novelist, Harriet Beecher Stowe, who wrote *Uncle Tom's Cabin*, an anti-slavery novel. The Beecher family was a progressive one, and Perkins was exposed to ideas about human rights and the need for social reform from an early age. When she was eighteen she studied Art and Design; afterwards, she earned a living teaching art and selling her artwork to local businesses. Such independence was unusual for a woman in those days.

Although Perkins knew that starting a family might compromise her career ambitions, she married Charles Stetson in 1884, and the following year they had a daughter, Katherine. Perkins suffered from postpartum depression, a condition which affects some women after they give birth. For two years she struggled with her illness before she was treated by Dr Weir Mitchell, a doctor famous for his 'rest cure' for such cases. (You can read more about Dr Mitchell's rest cure in the Background section.) After nine weeks, she was sent home with strict instructions to continue the treatment, which meant she had to stop writing, among other restrictions to her day-to-day life. She tried for three months, but her condition became worse. Eventually, she stopped the treatment and started writing again. She and Charles decided to separate in order for her to recover on her own. *The Yellow Wallpaper* is a semi-autobiographical account of this episode of her life.

She quickly recovered. Her improved mental health is clearly seen in her work: she became active in organisations whose goals were to improve society and women's lives. She started writing more, too, editing a publication called *The Bulletin*, and writing *The Yellow Wallpaper* during this period.

In 1893 she moved to New York, where she lived with her new husband, Houghton Gilman, until 1922. It was here that Perkins Gilman found fame as a writer and lecturer on a variety of subjects to do with the organization and reformation of society. Her most influential non-fiction books, *Women and Economics* (1898) and *The Home: Its Work and Influence* (1903) discussed issues that had not been tackled before. She argued that family life as it was structured then was not good for the well-being of women and that home life needed to change for women to realize their full potential as human beings.

It was also in New York that she recognized her limitations as a mother. She sent her daughter to live with Charles and his new wife, who she called Katherine's 'second mother', saying that she 'was fully as good as the first, better in some ways.' The conflict between a woman's roles in the home and at work was not just a topic of professional interest to her but something that profoundly affected her personal life.

Perkins Gilman's last years were as unconventional as the rest of her life. When her husband suddenly died in 1934, she had already been diagnosed with breast cancer. In 1935 she decided to kill herself rather than suffer, and even in this decision she showed her clear-minded logic and a determination to be free. In her suicide note she wrote: 'When all usefulness is over, when one is assured of an unavoidable and imminent death, it is the simplest of human rights to choose a quick and easy death in place of a slow and horrible one.'

Perkins Gilman influenced 20th century thought and politics through her original writings. Much of what she wrote paved the way for the feminist movement decades after her time. Interestingly, though, it is this one enigmatic story that has had the biggest influence of all.

About the story

The Yellow Wallpaper was written in just two days in June 1890 and first printed eighteen months later in *The New England Magazine*. Perkins Gilman's reasons for writing it were, as in much of her work, about changing people's minds. In this case, she had one reader very much in mind – the doctor who had treated her during her depression. 'The real purpose of the story was to reach Dr S. Weir Mitchell, and convince him of the error of his ways'. She sent him a copy.

People's responses to the story at the time were varied: one doctor protested that reading it would turn anyone mad, while another wrote to Perkins Gilman to let her know that it was the best description of insanity he had ever seen.

The real effect of the story on Dr Mitchell is difficult to know. Perkins Gilman believed it had worked: 'Many years later I was told that the great specialist had admitted to friends of his that he had altered his treatment of neurasthenia since reading *The Yellow Wallpaper*.' However, this is disputed by one writer who claims that the doctor was still promoting his rest cure 16 years later.

Background information

Postpartum psychosis

In modern terms, the symptoms that Perkins Gilman describes in *The Yellow Wallpaper* match those of postpartum psychosis, the name given to a group of psychiatric disorders that can occur in women after giving birth. These symptoms include mood swings, when patients quickly go from extreme happiness to terrible sadness or anger, and hallucinations, when they believe they are seeing things that do not exist. Another more common illness related to childbirth is postnatal depression, which is indicated by other symptoms described in the story, such as sadness, tiredness, irregular sleep, crying and anxiety.

Nervous energy

In the 19th century it was believed that neurological disorders like depression were caused when a person's 'nervous energy' was low. It was given the name 'neurasthenia' and, strangely, it was the wealthy middle and upper classes in big cities like New York who suffered from it most because it was they who were most exposed to the stresses and responsibility of modern city life. Consequently, it became quite fashionable to suffer from what was also called 'American nervousness'!

Women seemed to suffer from neurasthenia more than men. The reason given was that women were the weaker sex, according to the male-dominated medical profession at the time. In fact, it was believed in those days that women's brains were considerably more vulnerable to mental illness, and there were a number of psychiatric conditions common at the time that only affected women. These have since been discredited. One of these – *hysteria* – forms part of the story teller's vague diagnosis.

The terms *neurasthenia* and *hysteria* are no longer used today; instead, there are many recognised conditions that may have been described in this way, postnatal depression being one of them.

The rest cure

Silas Weir Mitchell was a prominent physician in late nineteenth-century American life. (A physician is an old-fashioned term for a doctor.) He became famous for developing a treatment for neurasthenia. Charlotte Perkins Gilman underwent Weir Mitchell's 'rest cure' when she was unwell, and in her story, the husband suggests that his wife be treated by Weir Mitchell, too. In fact, the treatment that is prescribed by her husband at home is basically the same. It consisted of a rich diet of undercooked meats, alcohol and tonics, which were medicines that were supposed to give energy, and complete rest from normal life duties such as looking after children or dealing with the house. It even discouraged any form of 'congenial' (pleasant and friendly) pastimes such as sewing or writing: 'Have but two hours' intellectual life a day. And never touch pen, brush or pencil as long as you live.'

Summary

It may help you to know something about what happens in the story before you read it. Don't worry, this summary does *not* tell you how the story ends!

The story describes the treatment of a woman for a psychological illness by her physician husband, John. The story is set in a large house in the countryside where the family spend the summer. It is told by the woman, whose name we are not told. John says that she is suffering from a 'temporary nervous depression' which started when their child was born. He insists that it is not serious but tells her not to do any work, including looking after their daughter, housekeeping or even writing, and to rest completely for the duration of the summer.

She is confined to a room at the top of the house, which John supposes must have been a nursery, or a room for small children to play and sleep in. The room has been chosen for its light and distance from the rest of the house but the story teller complains that she does not like the room for various reasons. John laughs at these complaints as trivial and unimportant, but they affect his wife profoundly.

Without stimulation or occupations of any kind, she has lots of time to think about her surroundings. She writes a sort of journal, or diary, despite her husband's instructions not to write. In her journal she describes the wallpaper in the room in detail.

Gradually, she starts imagining things and behaving strangely. As the last day of their stay approaches, her mental state deteriorates noticeably, her routine becomes irregular, and her behaviour unpredictable as the story builds towards its final climax.

Pre-reading activities

Key vocabulary

This section will help you familiarize yourself with some of the more specific vocabulary used in the story. You may want to use it to help you before you start reading, or as a revision exercise after you have finished the story.

Descriptive language

The story teller devotes a great deal of time to describing the appearance of her surroundings, especially the yellow wallpaper in her bedroom. Perkins Gilman uses many varied and colourful words to convey the colour, pattern, movement, texture, even the smell that the wallpaper gives off.

Synonyms for *horrible*

The story teller makes no secret of her hatred of the wallpaper. She describes it using many words that all share the dictionary definition of 'extremely unpleasant': *atrocious, foul, horrid, revolting, vicious*.

1 **Other adjectives have more specific meanings. Look at the definitions. Which of the adjectives is suggested in each of the sentences below?**

> **repellent** so unpleasant that you want to avoid it completely
> **lurid** bright and colourful in an ugly way
> **interminable** continuing for a long time in a boring or annoying way
> **grotesque** extremely ugly and strange
> **debased** having lost value or quality

1 You aren't seriously going out with that T-shirt on? They'll see you coming for miles!

2 The lecture was so dull – an hour and a half he talked for! I thought it would never end.

3 Terry doesn't just hate the taste of cheese. He can't even stand to be in the same room as it.

4 People don't realize just how much things are worth these days. If something breaks, they just throw it away.

5 What have you done to my face?! My eye's where my nose is supposed to be and my mouth is upside down!

Interior decoration

The interior decoration of the room the story teller is staying in is one of her central concerns. She goes into great detail trying to describe not just the wallpaper, but also the furniture, floors and windows.

2 Look at the words below and their definitions. Which words describe:

a) damage caused to interiors?
b) ways of improving interiors?
c) features of a room?

> **bedstead** the wooden or metal frame of a bed
> **fade** to gradually become paler or to lose colour
> **frieze** a line of decoration around the walls of a room or building
> **gouge** to cut long deep holes in something
> **hangings** a large piece of cloth that you hang on a wall for decoration
> **mopboard** a narrow piece of wood fixed to the bottom of the walls in a room
> **patch** an area that is different from what surrounds it
> **renovate** to make something old look new by repairing and improving it
> **splinter** to break into small sharp pieces, or to make something do this
> **stain** to leave a mark on something accidentally
> **tear off** to pull something so that it separates, or to become damaged in this way
> **whitewash** to paint walls or buildings white using whitewash

Wallpaper design: colour and pattern

3 **Read the text using the definitions below to help you. Why are traditional wallpaper designs so complicated and repetitive?**

Wallpaper in the 19th century typically featured **flamboyant** designs of plants, flowers or birds. **Patterns** were layered so that as well as the main **outline** there was a **fainter** design **dimly** visible underneath. Unlike the disordered natural world, however, wallpaper has to be **symmetrical** because of the way it is manufactured and put up in **strips**, or 'breadths'. A horizontal symmetry means the same pattern can be repeated across the wall of a room without having a break in the design. **Florid** patterns serve to hide the joins between breadths, and the **dull** sub-patterns help to confuse the eye for the same reason.

---

symmetrical a symmetrical shape or object has two halves that are exactly the same

strip a piece of something such as paper that is much longer than it is wide

pattern a set of lines, shapes, or colours that are repeated regularly

outline a line that shows the outer edge or shape of something

florid containing too much decoration

flamboyant brightly coloured or decorated

faint not strong or clear

dull not interesting, or not bright or shiny

dim not bright

---

4 **Which of the words above suggest that something is:**

a) clearly visible?
b) not clearly visible?

Things in the garden

The garden of the summer house captures the story teller's imagination. She describes it in detail as a place full of life.

5 **Look at the extracts. Match the words in bold (1–10) with their definitions (a–j).**

*I never saw such a garden – large and shady, full of box-bordered (1) **paths**, and lined with long grape-covered (2) **arbors** with seats under them.*

*There are (3) **hedges** and walls and gates that lock, and lots of separate little houses for the gardeners and people.*

*I don't like our room a bit. I wanted one downstairs that opened on the (4) **piazza**.*

*A lovely country, too, full of great (5) **elms** and velvet (6) **meadows**.*

*So I walk a little in the garden or down that lovely lane, sit on the (7) **porch** under the roses.*

*The outside pattern reminds one of a fungus ... a (8) **toadstool** in joints, an interminable string of toadstools ...*

*There are always new (9) **shoots** on the fungus.*

*It makes me think of all the yellow things I ever saw – not beautiful ones like (10) **buttercups**, but old foul, bad yellow things.*

---

a) a way from one place to another that people can walk along
b) shelters in a garden made by growing plants over a frame
c) plants with small bright yellow flowers
d) new parts growing on a plant
e) lines of bushes or small trees growing close together around a garden or field
f) large trees with round leaves
g) fields where grass and wild flowers grow
h) a wild fungus that is similar to a mushroom
i) a large open space which is paved with flat stones
j) an open area with a floor and a roof attached to the lower level of a house (US English, British English: *veranda*)

---

6 **Which of the words in the box are names of species of plant or fungus? Which are features of a garden?**

Verbs of movement

7 **Look at the definitions of these verbs of movement. Which of them involve moving from place to place?**

---

crawl to move along the ground on your hands and knees or with your body close to the ground
creep to move quietly and slowly
plunge to slope downwards suddenly
skulk to move around or to wait somewhere in a secret way, especially because you are going to do something bad
slant to move at an angle that is not 90 degrees, or to make something do this
somersault to form your body into a ball and roll forwards or backwards on the ground or in the air
sprawl to stretch over or across something in an ugly and untidy way
stir to move slightly after being still for a long time
stoop to bend the top half of your body downwards

> **tear about** to move somewhere very quickly, especially in an excited or uncontrolled way
>
> **trample** to put your feet down on someone or something in a heavy way that causes injury or damage
>
> **waddle** to walk with short steps that make your body move from side to side like a duck's body does when it walks
>
> **wallow** to lie down and roll around in water, dirt, or mud like a pig

8 **Complete the sentences with one of the verbs from 7 in the correct form.**

1 The view is stunning. The garden suddenly .... towards the ocean leaving a panorama of the coastline.

2 After three hours in front of the TV, he finally .... and went to make another cup of coffee.

3 Once she was sure that everyone had gone to sleep, Jasmine silently .... downstairs to see if her presents were under the tree.

4 The cows have escaped from the field again. This time they've .... all over my cabbages!

5 In the days before the trip she had to .... all over town buying walking boots, organizing travel insurance, getting visas ...

6 Honestly, I couldn't walk properly for days after that camel ride. I .... around Cairo like a complete idiot!

7 Some babies never learn to .... ; they go from sitting to walking in one step.

8 I'd never walk through that park at night: there are wild animals, ... in the shadows ... I'd be terrified!

9 **Complete these similes (1–6) with people and animals (a–f).**

1 to creep like a ....
2 to crawl like a ....
3 to trample through the forest like a ....
4 to waddle like a ....
5 to tear about like a ....
6 to wallow like a ....

a herd of elephants
b bunch of schoolchildren
c cat
d hippopotamus
e baby
f duck

Abstract nouns

An abstract noun is a word that describes something that you cannot see or touch. It refers to a quality, idea, or feeling rather than to a person, animal, place, or thing. Perkins Gilman uses a number of unusual abstract nouns in *The Yellow Wallpaper*.

10 Use abstract nouns from the list below to complete the sentences.

---

burden a serious or difficult responsibility that you have to deal with

deceit dishonest behaviour that is intended to trick someone

defiance refusal to obey a person or rule

derision the opinion that someone or something is stupid, unimportant, or useless

distraction something that gets your attention and prevents you from concentrating on something else

fatuity *uncommon*: total stupidity

felicity *formal*: great happiness

hypothesis an idea that attempts to explain something but has not yet been tested or proved to be correct

peculiarity something strange in the way that a person or animal behaves, or in their appearance

sin an action or way of behaving that you think is wrong

undertaking something difficult or complicated that you do

whim a sudden feeling that you must have or must do something, often something not important

---

1 He's acting a bit strangely. Have you noticed any .... in his behaviour recently?

2 The man's utter .... is seen in these high-sounding but essentially meaningless words.

3 The next politician to stand up was even less popular. There were shouts of .... from the audience.

4 The honeymooning couple were in a state of marital .... as they drove off into the sunset.

5 The captain had prisoners shot at random. They were executed at his .... , which created great tensions and fear among the camp population.

6 We have work to do and it is essential that there are no ....

7 Men say they are willing to share the .... of domestic work with women. Whether they mean it or not is another matter.

8 She spoke to her boss with a tone of .... There was no way she was going to apologize.

9   The whole relationship was based on lies and ....

10   It's a .... the way she spends money. And the number of
     pairs of shoes she's got!

11   Our findings support the .... that these patients are at
     increased risk of heart disease.

12   Organizing a wedding is a major ....

Main themes

Before you read the story, you may want to think about some of its
main themes. The questions will help you think about the story as you
are reading it for the first time. There is more discussion of the main
themes in the *Literary analysis* section after the story.

Men's and women's roles

The two main characters are husband and wife, but they are also doctor
and patient. In the nineteenth century, the traditional relationships
between both sets of roles were hardly ever challenged. Just as the
husband had authority over his wife and made the important decisions
in the family, so a doctor's expert opinion was never questioned. John,
the physician husband, represents both these characters in one person.
Men's duties were to provide financial stability and women's duties
were to bring up the children and take care of the household.

11 As you read the story, ask yourself:

a) Why does the story teller accept her roles of wife and patient and
    her husband's authority?

b) Does she show any unwillingness to play these roles? How?

c) What general impressions do you get from the story about marriage
    in the late 19th century in the United States?

Fancy and sense

Fancy is an important concept in the story. As a verb, *fancy* is used
today in informal British English to mean to want, as in 'I fancy an ice
cream'. It has an old-fashioned use in the story meaning to imagine
and as a noun to refer to the mental faculty of imagination, the ability
to create visual images, stories and fantasies.

Fancy was seen as the product of the female brain; it referred to
an imagination that was silly and not important, nothing more than
child's play. It was held in contrast with the male faculties of *will* and
good sense – qualities seen as important for the serious world of work.

12 As you read the story, ask yourself:

a) What role does fancy play in the story teller's life?

b) What is her attitude to fancy? And her husband's?

A Gothic tale?

Gothic literature was well established by Perkins Gilman's time. It is a type of fiction that romanticizes the horror genre, and is most famous in works like Mary Shelley's *Frankenstein* and Bram Stoker's *Dracula*. However, not all Gothic fiction includes monsters and castles haunted by ghosts and demons. Edgar Allen Poe had developed the genre by confining the terror to the mind of the main character in psychological horror stories such as *The Fall of the House of Usher*. Often, it is unclear whether the terror is real or imagined. In other words, the horror is generated from not knowing whether a character should be afraid of something outside of themselves or should fear their own dark imaginings.

Gothic literature typically includes an isolated location, usually an old building, which is far from civilization and holds strange secrets from a dark and shadowy past. The main character feels alone with no one to share their worries with; they may be unable to escape.

13 As you read the story, ask yourself:

a) Are there any Gothic elements in the story?

b) Do you think the mansion is haunted in any way?

Writing as therapy

This semi-autobiographical story talks about itself; that is to say, the writing of the story is one of its themes. In the same way that Perkins Gilman wrote *The Yellow Wallpaper* as a way of understanding and coming to terms with her depression and anger at being treated so poorly, so her story teller feels a need to write.

14 As you read the story, ask yourself:

a) How does writing contradict the treatment that her husband prescribes?

b) In what ways does writing seem to help?

The Yellow Wallpaper

by Charlotte Perkins Gilman

It is very **seldom** that mere ordinary people like John and myself secure ancestral halls[1] for the summer.

A colonial **mansion**, a hereditary estate[2], I would say a haunted house, and reach the height of romantic felicity – but that would be asking too much of fate!

Still I will proudly declare that there is something queer[3] about it.

Else, why should it be let so cheaply? And why have stood so long **untenanted**?

John laughs at me, of course, but one expects that in marriage.

John is practical in the extreme. He has no patience with faith, an intense horror of superstition, and he **scoffs** openly at any talk of things not to be felt and seen and put down in figures.

John is a physician, and PERHAPS – (I would not say it to a living soul, of course, but this is dead paper and a great relief to my mind) – PERHAPS that is one reason I do not get well faster.

You see he does not believe I am sick!

And what can one do?

If a physician of high standing, and one's own husband, assures friends and relatives that there is really nothing the matter with one but temporary nervous depression – a slight hysterical tendency – what is one to do?

My brother is also a physician, and also of high standing, and he says the same thing.

So I take phosphates or phosphites – whichever it is, and tonics, and journeys, and air, and exercise, and am absolutely forbidden to 'work' until I am well again.

1 a house that has belonged to a rich family for several generations
2 a house and land officially passed from a parent to their child
3 *old-fashioned:* strange

Personally, I disagree with their ideas.

Personally, I believe that congenial work, with excitement and change, would do me good.

But what is one to do?

I did write for a while in spite of them; but it *does* exhaust me a good deal – having to be so **sly** about it, or else meet with heavy opposition.

I sometimes fancy that in my condition if I had less opposition and more society and stimulus – but John says the very worst thing I can do is to think about my condition, and I confess it always makes me feel bad.

So I will **let it alone** and talk about the house.

The most beautiful place! It is quite alone, standing well back from the road, quite three miles from the village. It makes me think of English places that you read about, for there are hedges and walls and gates that lock, and lots of separate little houses for the gardeners and people.

There is a *delicious* garden! I never saw such a garden – large and **shady**, full of box-bordered paths, and lined with long grape-covered arbors with seats under them.

There were greenhouses, too, but they are all broken now.

There was some legal trouble, I believe, something about the heirs and coheirs[4]; anyhow, the place has been empty for years.

That spoils my ghostliness, I am afraid, but I don't care – there is something strange about the house – I can feel it.

I even said so to John one moonlight evening, but he said what I felt was a *draught*[5], and shut the window.

I get unreasonably angry with John sometimes. I'm sure I never used to be so sensitive. I think it is due to this nervous condition.

But John says if I feel so, I shall neglect proper self-control; so I take pains to control myself – before him, at least, and that makes me very tired.

I don't like our room a bit. I wanted one downstairs that opened on the piazza and had roses all over the window, and

4 people who will receive money, property, or a title when another person dies
5 cold air that blows into a room and makes you feel uncomfortable

such pretty old-fashioned chintz hangings! but John would not hear of it.

He said there was only one window and not room for two beds, and no near room for him if he took another.

He is very careful and loving, and hardly lets me stir without special direction.

I have a schedule prescription for each hour in the day; he takes all care from me, and so I feel basely ungrateful[6] not to value it more.

He said we came here solely on my account, that I was to have perfect rest and all the air I could get. 'Your exercise depends on your strength, my dear,' said he, 'and your food somewhat on your appetite; but air you can absorb all the time.' So we took the nursery at the top of the house.

It is a big, airy room, the whole floor nearly, with windows that look all ways, and air and sunshine galore[7]. It was nursery first and then playroom and gymnasium, I should judge; for the windows are barred for little children, and there are rings and things in the walls.

The paint and paper look as if a boys' school had used it. It is stripped off – the paper – in great patches all around the head of my bed, about as far as I can reach, and in a great place on the other side of the room low down. I never saw a worse paper in my life.

One of those sprawling flamboyant patterns committing every artistic sin.

It is dull enough to confuse the eye in following, pronounced enough to constantly irritate and provoke study, and when you follow the lame uncertain curves for a little distance they suddenly commit suicide – plunge off at **outrageous** angles, destroy themselves in unheard-of contradictions.

The color is repellent, almost revolting; a **smouldering** unclean yellow, strangely faded by the slow-turning sunlight.

---

6 not showing appreciation for someone's kindness
7 (adjective used after nouns) used for emphasizing how large an amount or quantity is

It is a dull yet lurid orange in some places, a sickly sulphur[8] tint in others.

No wonder the children hated it! I should hate it myself if I had to live in this room long.

There comes John, and I must put this away, – he hates to have me write a word.

———

We have been here two weeks, and I haven't felt like writing before, since that first day.

I am sitting by the window now, up in this atrocious nursery, and there is nothing to hinder my writing as much as I please, save lack of strength.

John is away all day, and even some nights when his cases are serious.

I am glad my case is not serious!

But these nervous troubles are dreadfully depressing.

John does not know how much I really suffer. He knows there is no *reason* to suffer, and that satisfies him.

Of course it is only nervousness. It does weigh on me so not to do my duty in any way!

I meant to be such a help to John, such a real rest and comfort, and here I am a comparative burden already!

Nobody would believe what an effort it is to do what little I am able, – to dress and entertain, and order things.

It is fortunate Mary is so good with the baby. Such a dear baby!

And yet I *cannot* be with him, it makes me so nervous.

I suppose John never was nervous in his life. He laughs at me so about this wallpaper!

At first he meant to repaper the room, but afterwards he said that I was letting it get the better of me[9], and that nothing was worse for a nervous patient than to give way to such fancies.

---

8 a yellow chemical element that has a strong smell, used for making medicines and explosives

9 if an emotion or feeling gets the better of you, it is too strong for you to control and it makes you do something that you did not intend to do

He said that after the wallpaper was changed it would be the heavy bedstead, and then the barred windows, and then that gate at the head of the stairs, and so on.

'You know the place is doing you good,' he said, 'and really, dear, I don't care to renovate the house just for a three months' rental.'

'Then do let us go downstairs,' I said, 'there are such pretty rooms there.'

Then he took me in his arms and called me a blessed little goose[10], and said he would go down to the cellar, if I wished, and have it whitewashed into the bargain.

But he is right enough about the beds and windows and things.

It is an airy and comfortable room as any one need wish, and, of course, I would not be so silly as to make him uncomfortable just for a whim.

I'm really getting quite fond of the big room, all but that horrid paper.

Out of one window I can see the garden, those mysterious deepshaded arbors, the riotous[11] old-fashioned flowers, and bushes and **gnarly** trees.

Out of another I get a lovely view of the bay and a little private **wharf** belonging to the estate. There is a beautiful shaded lane that runs down there from the house. I always fancy I see people walking in these numerous paths and arbors, but John has cautioned me not to give way to fancy in the least. He says that with my imaginative power and habit of story-making, a nervous weakness like mine is sure to lead to all manner of excited fancies, and that I ought to use my will and good sense to **check** the tendency. So I try.

I think sometimes that if I were only well enough to write a little it would relieve the press of ideas and rest me.

But I find I get pretty tired when I try.

10 *old-fashioned*: a term of endearment that you say to someone you love
11 *literary*: full of life, colour and movement

It is so discouraging not to have any advice and companionship about my work. When I get really well, John says we will ask Cousin Henry and Julia down for a long visit; but he says he would as soon put fireworks in my pillow-case as to let me have those stimulating people about now.

I wish I could get well faster.

But I must not think about that. This paper looks to me as if it *knew* what a vicious influence it had!

There is a **recurrent** spot where the pattern lolls[12] like a broken neck and two **bulbous** eyes stare at you upside down.

I get positively angry with the impertinence of it and the everlastingness. Up and down and sideways they crawl, and those absurd, unblinking eyes are everywhere. There is one place where two breadths didn't match, and the eyes go all up and down the line, one a little higher than the other.

I never saw so much expression in an inanimate thing before, and we all know how much expression they have! I used to lie awake as a child and get more entertainment and terror out of blank walls and plain furniture than most children could find in a toy store.

I remember what a kindly **wink** the **knobs** of our big, old bureau[13] used to have, and there was one chair that always seemed like a strong friend.

I used to feel that if any of the other things looked too fierce I could always hop into that chair and be safe.

The furniture in this room is no worse than inharmonious[14], however, for we had to bring it all from downstairs. I suppose when this was used as a playroom they had to take the nursery things out, and no wonder! I never saw such **ravages** as the children have made here.

The wallpaper, as I said before, is torn off in spots, and it sticketh closer than a brother[15] – they must have had perseverance as well as hatred.

12 if your tongue or your head lolls, it hangs down in an uncontrolled way
13 *US English*: a chest of drawers (in British English, a type of desk)
14 not combining well together
15 an expression from the bible. Here it is used to emphasize how difficult it is to get the wallpaper off the wall.

Then the floor is scratched and gouged and splintered, the **plaster** itself is dug out here and there, and this great heavy bed which is all we found in the room, looks as if it had been through the wars.

But I don't mind it a bit – only the paper.

There comes John's sister. Such a dear girl as she is, and so careful of me! I must not let her find me writing.

She is a perfect and enthusiastic housekeeper, and hopes for no better profession. I verily[16] believe she thinks it is the writing which made me sick!

But I can write when she is out, and see her a long way off from these windows.

There is one that commands the road, a lovely shaded winding road, and one that just looks off over the country. A lovely country, too, full of great elms and velvet meadows.

This wallpaper has a kind of sub-pattern in a different **shade**, a particularly irritating one, for you can only see it in certain lights, and not clearly then.

But in the places where it isn't faded and where the sun is just so – I can see a strange, provoking, formless sort of figure, that seems to skulk about behind that silly and **conspicuous** front design.

There's sister on the stairs!

———

Well, the Fourth of July[17] is over! The people are gone and I am tired out. John thought it might do me good to see a little company, so we just had mother and Nellie and the children down for a week.

Of course I didn't do a thing. Jennie sees to everything now.

But it tired me all the same.

John says if I don't pick up faster he shall send me to Weir Mitchell in the fall[18].

16 *old-fashioned*: used for emphasizing that something is true
17 a holiday in the United States, when Americans celebrate independence from Great Britain
18 *US English*: autumn

But I don't want to go there at all. I had a friend who was in his hands once, and she says he is just like John and my brother, only more so!

Besides, it is such an undertaking to go so far.

I don't feel as if it was **worthwhile** to turn my hand over for anything, and I'm getting dreadfully **fretful** and querulous[19].

I cry at nothing, and cry most of the time.

Of course I don't when John is here, or anybody else, but when I am alone.

And I am alone a good deal just now. John is kept in town very often by serious cases, and Jennie is good and lets me alone when I want her to.

So I walk a little in the garden or down that lovely lane, sit on the porch under the roses, and lie down up here a good deal.

I'm getting really fond of the room in spite of the wallpaper. Perhaps *because* of the wallpaper.

It dwells[20] in my mind so!

I lie here on this great immovable bed – it is nailed down, I believe – and follow that pattern about by the hour. It is as good as gymnastics, I assure you. I start, we'll say, at the bottom, down in the corner over there where it has not been touched, and I determine for the thousandth time that I *will* follow that pointless pattern to some sort of a conclusion.

I know a little of the principle of design, and I know this thing was not arranged on any laws of radiation, or alternation, or repetition, or symmetry, or anything else that I ever heard of.

It is repeated, of course, by the breadths, but not otherwise.

Looked at in one way each breadth stands alone, the bloated curves and flourishes[21] – a kind of 'debased Romanesque[22]'with delirium tremens[23] – go waddling up and down in isolated columns of fatuity.

19 *literary*: a querulous person complains often and in a way that annoys other people
20 *literary*: if something such as a feeling dwells in a place, it exists and is very noticeable there
21 curved lines added to letters when you are writing to make them look more attractive
22 *art*: belonging to a style of building that was common in Europe from about AD 900 to 1200
23 a severe reaction that alcoholics experience after they stop drinking that involves violent shaking

But, on the other hand, they connect diagonally, and the sprawling outlines run off in great slanting waves of optic horror, like a lot of wallowing seaweeds in full chase.

The whole thing goes horizontally, too, at least it seems so, and I exhaust myself in trying to distinguish the order of its going in that direction.

They have used a horizontal breadth for a frieze, and that adds wonderfully to the confusion.

There is one end of the room where it is almost intact, and there, when the crosslights fade and the low sun shines directly upon it, I can almost fancy radiation after all, – the interminable grotesques seem to form around a common centre and rush off in headlong plunges of equal distraction.

It makes me tired to follow it. I will take a **nap** I guess.

———

I don't know why I should write this.

I don't want to.

I don't feel able.

And I know John would think it absurd. But I must say what I feel and think in some way – it is such a relief!

But the effort is getting to be greater than the relief.

Half the time now I am awfully lazy, and lie down ever so much.

John says I mustn't lose my strength, and has me take cod liver oil and lots of tonics and things, to say nothing of ale and wine and **rare** meat.

Dear John! He loves me very dearly, and hates to have me sick. I tried to have a real **earnest** reasonable talk with him the other day, and tell him how I wish he would let me go and make a visit to Cousin Henry and Julia.

But he said I wasn't able to go, nor able to stand it after I got there; and I did not make out a very good case for myself, for I was crying before I had finished.

It is getting to be a great effort for me to think straight. Just this nervous weakness I suppose.

And dear John gathered me up in his arms, and just carried me upstairs and laid me on the bed, and sat by me and read to me till it tired my head.

He said I was his darling and his comfort and all he had, and that I must take care of myself for his sake, and keep well.

He says no one but myself can help me out of it, that I must use my will and self-control and not let any silly fancies run away with me.

There's one comfort, the baby is well and happy, and does not have to occupy this nursery with the horrid wallpaper.

If we had not used it, that blessed child would have! What a fortunate escape! Why, I wouldn't have a child of mine, an impressionable little thing, live in such a room for worlds.

I never thought of it before, but it is lucky that John kept me here after all, I can stand it so much easier than a baby, you see.

Of course I never mention it to them any more – I am too wise, – but I keep watch of it all the same.

There are things in that paper that nobody knows but me, or ever will.

Behind that outside pattern the dim shapes get clearer every day.

It is always the same shape, only very numerous.

And it is like a woman stooping down and creeping about behind that pattern. I don't like it a bit. I wonder – I begin to think – I wish John would take me away from here!

———

It is so hard to talk with John about my case, because he is so wise, and because he loves me so.

But I tried it last night.

It was moonlight. The moon shines in all around just as the sun does.

I hate to see it sometimes, it creeps so slowly, and always comes in by one window or another.

John was asleep and I hated to waken him, so I kept still and watched the moonlight on that undulating wallpaper till I felt creepy.

The faint figure behind seemed to shake the pattern, just as if she wanted to get out.

I got up softly and went to feel and see if the paper *did* move, and when I came back John was awake.

'What is it, little girl?' he said. "Don't go walking about like that—you'll get cold.'

I thought it was a good time to talk, so I told him that I really was not gaining here, and that I wished he would take me away.

'Why darling!' said he, 'our **lease** will be up in three weeks, and I can't see how to leave before.

'The repairs are not done at home, and I cannot possibly leave town just now. Of course if you were in any danger, I could and would, but you really are better, dear, whether you can see it or not. I am a doctor, dear, and I know. You are gaining flesh and color, your appetite is better, I feel really much easier about you.'

'I don't weigh a bit more,' said I, 'nor as much; and my appetite may be better in the evening when you are here, but it is worse in the morning when you are away!'

'Bless her little heart!' said he with a big **hug**, 'she shall be as sick as she pleases! But now let's improve the shining hours by going to sleep, and talk about it in the morning!'

'And you won't go away?' I asked **gloomily**.

'Why, how can I, dear? It is only three weeks more and then we will take a nice little trip of a few days while Jennie is getting the house ready. Really dear you are better!'

'Better in body perhaps – ' I began, and stopped short, for he sat up straight and looked at me with such a stern, reproachful[24] look that I could not say another word.

'My darling,' said he, 'I beg of you, for my sake and for our child's sake, as well as for your own, that you will never for one instant let that idea enter your mind! There is nothing so dangerous, so fascinating, to a temperament like yours. It is a false and foolish fancy. Can you not trust me as a physician when I tell you so?'

So of course I said no more on that score, and we went to sleep before long. He thought I was asleep first, but I wasn't, and lay there for hours trying to decide whether that front pattern and the back pattern really did move together or separately.

---

24 expressing criticism or disappointment in a way that is intended to make someone feel ashamed

On a pattern like this, by daylight, there is a lack of sequence, a defiance of law, that is a constant irritant to a normal mind.

The color is hideous enough, and unreliable enough, and infuriating enough, but the pattern is torturing.

You think you have mastered it, but just as you get well underway in following, it turns a back-somersault and there you are. It slaps you in the face, knocks you down, and tramples upon you. It is like a bad dream.

The outside pattern is a florid arabesque[25], reminding one of a fungus. If you can imagine a toadstool in joints, an interminable string of toadstools, budding and sprouting in endless convolutions[26] – why, that is something like it.

That is, sometimes!

There is one marked peculiarity about this paper, a thing nobody seems to notice but myself, and that is that it changes as the light changes.

When the sun shoots in through the east window – I always watch for that first long, straight ray – it changes so quickly that I never can quite believe it.

That is why I watch it always.

By moonlight – the moon shines in all night when there is a moon – I wouldn't know it was the same paper.

At night in any kind of light, in twilight, candle light, lamplight, and worst of all by moonlight, it becomes bars! The outside pattern I mean, and the woman behind it is as plain as can be.

I didn't realize for a long time what the thing was that showed behind, that dim sub-pattern, but now I am quite sure it is a woman.

By daylight she is **subdued**, quiet. I fancy it is the pattern that keeps her so still. It is so puzzling. It keeps me quiet by the hour.

I lie down ever so much now. John says it is good for me, and to sleep all I can.

Indeed he started the habit by making me lie down for an hour after each meal.

25 *art*: a pattern of curved lines used as decoration
26 *formal*: a complicated detail or shape

It is a very bad habit I am convinced, for you see I don't sleep.

And that cultivates deceit, for I don't tell them I'm awake—O no!

The fact is I am getting a little afraid of John.

He seems very queer sometimes, and even Jennie has an inexplicable look.

It strikes me occasionally, just as a scientific hypothesis, – that perhaps it is the paper!

I have watched John when he did not know I was looking, and come into the room suddenly on the most innocent excuses, and I've caught him several times *looking at the paper*! And Jennie too. I caught Jennie with her hand on it once.

She didn't know I was in the room, and when I asked her in a quiet, a very quiet voice, with the most restrained manner possible, what she was doing with the paper – she turned around as if she had been caught stealing, and looked quite angry – asked me why I should frighten her so!

Then she said that the paper stained everything it touched, that she had found yellow smooches[27] on all my clothes and John's, and she wished we would be more careful!

Did not that sound innocent? But I know she was studying that pattern, and I am determined that nobody shall find it out but myself!

––––––

Life is very much more exciting now than it used to be. You see I have something more to expect, to look forward to, to watch. I really do eat better, and am more quiet than I was.

John is so pleased to see me improve! He laughed a little the other day, and said I seemed to be **flourishing** in spite of my wallpaper.

I turned it off with a laugh. I had no intention of telling him it was *because* of the wallpaper – he would make fun of me. He might even want to take me away.

I don't want to leave now until I have found it out. There is a week more, and I think that will be enough.

27 *unusual, more commonly 'smear' or 'smudge'*: a dirty mark made by rubbing something such as dirt

I'm feeling ever so much better! I don't sleep much at night, for it is so interesting to watch developments; but I sleep a good deal in the daytime.

In the daytime it is tiresome and perplexing.

There are always new shoots on the fungus, and new shades of yellow all over it. I cannot keep count of them, though I have tried conscientiously.

It is the strangest yellow, that wallpaper! It makes me think of all the yellow things I ever saw – not beautiful ones like buttercups, but old foul, bad yellow things.

But there is something else about that paper – the smell! I noticed it the moment we came into the room, but with so much air and sun it was not bad. Now we have had a week of fog and rain, and whether the windows are open or not, the smell is here.

It creeps all over the house.

I find it hovering in the dining-room, skulking in the parlor, hiding in the hall, lying in wait for me on the stairs.

It gets into my hair.

Even when I go to ride, if I turn my head suddenly and surprise it – there is that smell!

Such a peculiar odor, too! I have spent hours in trying to analyze it, to find what it smelled like.

It is not bad – at first, and very gentle, but quite the subtlest, most enduring odor I ever met.

In this damp weather it is awful, I wake up in the night and find it hanging over me.

It used to disturb me at first. I thought seriously of burning the house – to reach the smell.

But now I am used to it. The only thing I can think of that it is like is the *color* of the paper! A yellow smell.

There is a very funny mark on this wall, low down, near the mopboard. A streak that runs round the room. It goes behind every piece of furniture, except the bed, a long, straight, even *smooch*, as if it had been rubbed over and over.

I wonder how it was done and who did it, and what they did it for. Round and round and round – round and round and round – it makes me dizzy!

———

I really have discovered something at last.

Through watching so much at night, when it changes so, I have finally found out.

The front pattern *does* move – and no wonder! The woman behind shakes it!

Sometimes I think there are a great many women behind, and sometimes only one, and she crawls around fast, and her crawling shakes it all over.

Then in the very bright spots she keeps still, and in the very shady spots she just takes hold of the bars and shakes them hard.

And she is all the time trying to climb through. But nobody could climb through that pattern – it strangles so; I think that is why it has so many heads.

They get through, and then the pattern strangles them off and turns them upside down, and makes their eyes white!

If those heads were covered or taken off it would not be half so bad.

———

I think that woman gets out in the daytime!

And I'll tell you why – privately – I've seen her!

I can see her out of every one of my windows!

It is the same woman, I know, for she is always creeping, and most women do not creep by daylight.

I see her on that long road under the trees, creeping along, and when a carriage comes she hides under the blackberry vines.

I don't blame her a bit. It must be very humiliating to be caught creeping by daylight!

I always lock the door when I creep by daylight. I can't do it at night, for I know John would suspect something at once.

And John is so queer now, that I don't want to irritate him. I wish he would take another room! Besides, I don't want anybody to get that woman out at night but myself.

I often wonder if I could see her out of all the windows at once.

But, turn as fast as I can, I can only see out of one at one time.

And though I always see her, she *may* be able to creep faster than I can turn!

I have watched her sometimes away off in the open country, creeping as fast as a cloud shadow in a high wind.

———

If only that top pattern could be gotten off from the under one! I mean to try it, little by little.

I have found out another funny thing, but I shan't tell it this time! It does not do to trust people too much.

There are only two more days to get this paper off, and I believe John is beginning to notice. I don't like the look in his eyes.

And I heard him ask Jennie a lot of professional questions about me. She had a very good report to give.

She said I slept a good deal in the daytime.

John knows I don't sleep very well at night, for all I'm so quiet!

He asked me all sorts of questions, too, and pretended to be very loving and kind.

As if I couldn't **see through** him!

Still, I don't wonder he acts so, sleeping under this paper for three months.

It only interests me, but I feel sure John and Jennie are secretly affected by it.

———

Hurrah! This is the last day, but it is enough. John is to stay in town over night, and won't be out until this evening.

Jennie wanted to sleep with me -- the sly thing! but I told her I should undoubtedly rest better for a night all alone.

That was clever, for really I wasn't alone a bit! As soon as it was moonlight and that poor thing began to crawl and shake the pattern, I got up and ran to help her.

I pulled and she shook, I shook and she pulled, and before morning we had **peeled off** yards of that paper.

A strip about as high as my head and half around the room.

And then when the sun came and that awful pattern began to laugh at me, I declared I would finish it to-day!

We go away to-morrow, and they are moving all my furniture down again to leave things as they were before.

Jennie looked at the wall in amazement, but I told her merrily that I did it **out of pure spite** at the vicious thing.

She laughed and said she wouldn't mind doing it herself, but I must not get tired.

How she betrayed herself that time!

But I am here, and no person touches this paper but me – not *alive*!

She tried to get me out of the room – it was too patent[28]! But I said it was so quiet and empty and clean now that I believed I would lie down again and sleep all I could; and not to wake me even for dinner – I would call when I woke.

So now she is gone, and the servants are gone, and the things are gone, and there is nothing left but that great bedstead nailed down, with the canvas mattress we found on it.

We shall sleep downstairs to-night, and take the boat home to-morrow.

I quite enjoy the room, now it is bare again.

How those children did tear about here!

This bedstead is fairly **gnawed**!

But I must get to work.

I have locked the door and thrown the key down into the front path.

I don't want to go out, and I don't want to have anybody come in, till John comes.

I want to **astonish** him.

I've got a rope up here that even Jennie did not find. If that woman does get out, and tries to get away, I can tie her!

But I forgot I could not reach far without anything to stand on!

This bed will *not* move!

28 (*normally before a noun*) extremely obvious

I tried to lift and push it until I was lame, and then I got so angry I bit off a little piece at one corner – but it hurt my teeth.

Then I peeled off all the paper I could reach standing on the floor. It sticks horribly and the pattern just enjoys it! All those strangled heads and bulbous eyes and waddling fungus growths just shriek with derision!

I am getting angry enough to do something desperate. To jump out of the window would be admirable exercise, but the bars are too strong even to try.

Besides I wouldn't do it. Of course not. I know well enough that a step like that is **improper** and might be misconstrued[29].

I don't like to *look* out of the windows even – there are so many of those creeping women, and they creep so fast.

I wonder if they all come out of that wallpaper as I did?

But I am securely fastened now by my well-hidden rope – you don't get *me* out in the road there!

I suppose I shall have to get back behind the pattern when it comes night, and that is hard!

It is so pleasant to be out in this great room and creep around as I please!

I don't want to go outside. I won't, even if Jennie asks me to.

For outside you have to creep on the ground, and everything is green instead of yellow.

But here I can creep smoothly on the floor, and my shoulder just fits in that long smooch around the wall, so I cannot lose my way.

Why there's John at the door!

It is no use, young man, you can't open it!

How he does call and **pound**!

Now he's crying for an **axe**.

It would be a shame to break down that beautiful door!

'John dear!' said I in the gentlest voice, 'the key is down by the front steps, under a plantain leaf!'

That silenced him for a few moments.

29 *formal*: to understand something wrongly

Then he said – very quietly indeed, 'Open the door, my darling!'

'I can't,' said I. 'The key is down by the front door under a plantain leaf!'

And then I said it again, several times, very gently and slowly, and said it so often that he had to go and see, and he got it of course, and came in. He stopped short by the door.

'What is the matter?' he cried. 'For God's sake, what are you doing!'

I kept on creeping just the same, but I looked at him over my shoulder.

'I've got out at last,'said I, 'in spite of you and Jane. And I've pulled off most of the paper, so you can't put me back!'

Now why should that man have **fainted**? But he did, and right across my path by the wall, so that I had to creep over him every time!

Post-reading activities

Understanding the story

Use these questions to help you check that you have understood the story.

Their arrival and first impressions

1 Why is it unusual for 'ordinary people' like the story teller and her husband to stay in a place like the colonial mansion?
2 How does the woman's opinion about her health differ from her husband's? Why is his opinion accepted as the correct one?
3 Why might the house feel ghostly?
4 Why is she unhappy about the room John has chosen for her? What room did she want?
5 Why does she feel that she should be grateful to John?
6 Why did John choose the upstairs bedroom for her?
7 She explains various reasons why she does not like the wallpaper. Name three of them.

Two weeks later

8 Why is John absent so often from the house?
9 John gives various reasons not to repaper the room despite her wishes. What are they?
10 Describe the two views from the windows in the room.
11 What prevents her from writing more?
12 Why does she talk about furniture from her childhood? In what way is the wallpaper similar to this furniture, in her mind?
13 What happens on the Fourth of July?
14 Why is she reluctant to go to Dr Weir Mitchell?
15 Why does she start to appreciate the wallpaper?
16 Draw a section of the wallpaper as you imagine it from the descriptions.

Seeing things

17 What does she start to see behind the pattern?
18 What does she talk to John about in the middle of the night?
19 John gets angry with her when she says that she is feeling 'Better in body perhaps –'. What do you understand by the comment? Why is he angry?

20 How does the wallpaper change at night?
21 What evidence is there that she stops trusting her husband?
22 How does her attitude to staying there until the end of the summer change?
23 What is her discovery?
24 Her madness becomes clear in her own description of her own behaviour. What does she do that shows that she is mentally unwell?
25 What do you understand when she says: 'I wonder if they all come out of that wallpaper as I did?'
26 What image are we left with in the last line of the story? Describe the scene.

Language study

Grammar

I wish and if only

Present situations

The story teller finds it very difficult to talk to her husband about her feelings, but she is free to write about her desires and wishes in secret. She is not happy in her present condition and she uses I wish and if only to express how she would like to see it change.

> I **wish** I **could** get well faster.

(real situation: I'm getting better very slowly.)

Use I wish and if only + **past simple** to express wishes and desires about the present.

> I'm not feeling well and I can't write → If only I **were** well enough to write a little

Notice that the verb after I is were. Both I wish / If only I **was**... and I wish / If only I **were**... are possible. Was is generally more frequent in informal speech.

Use if only/I wish + **would** to complain about other people's actions and reactions.

> I don't like it a bit. I wonder – I begin to think – I wish John **would take** me away from here!

> Then she said that the paper stained everything it touched, that she had found yellow smooches on all my clothes and John's, and she wished we **would be** more careful!

Past situations

We use *wish* and *if only* + past perfect (*had* + past participle) when we regret past actions:

> **If only** I hadn't cried when I tried to talk John into letting me visit Cousin Henry and Julia. (= I cried when I talked to John and I'm not happy that I did.)

> I **wish** John **had chosen** a better room than this. (= John chose this room and I don't like his choice.)

Note: *If only* can convey a stronger feeling of regret or longing than *I wish*. It is more literary and less common in everyday usage.

1 Use *wish* or *if only* to express the negative feelings suggested in these sentences.

e.g. My dad cooks for us. We don't eat enough vegetables.
I wish *we ate more vegetables.* (or) I wish *Dad cooked more vegetables for us.*

1 This shirt looks terrible. I didn't iron it this morning.
I wish I had

2 I went for a walk yesterday in the rain. Now I have a cold.
If only I hadn't

3 Harriet doesn't have a jacket with her at the football match. It's freezing.
Harriet wishes she

4 The Taylors' house wasn't insured. The fire destroyed everything they owned.
If only the Taylors

5 Richard is quite short. He loves basketball but he can't play competitively.
Richard

6 My brother is always playing loud music when I'm watching TV. It's so annoying!
I

7 I didn't study Science at school. Now I want to be an astronomer.
If

8 You left the car unlocked. Someone stole it!
If

Reporting direct speech

The conversations between the story teller and her controlling husband play an important role in the story. Perkins Gilman limits herself to simple reporting verbs such as *say*, *ask*, and *tell*, as you might expect in a person's private diary. Dialogues are usually reported indirectly, such as in this extract:

> *There is something strange about the house—I can feel it. I even **said** so to John one moonlight evening, but he **said** what I felt was a draught, and shut the window.*

However, when Perkins Gilman wants to focus attention on important conversations, she uses direct speech. The reporting verbs often come in the middle of the direct speech:

> *'Bless her little heart!' **said John** with a big hug*

> *'You know the place is doing you good,' **he said**, 'and really, dear, I don't care to renovate the house just for a three months' rental.'*

> *'Your exercise depends on your strength, my dear,'**said he,** 'and your food somewhat on your appetite; but air you can absorb all the time.'*

The order of the verb and subject can be inverted, from *John said* to *said John*. This is normally only possible in the middle or at the end of the direct speech. It is most common with the verb *said*, but can be used with other verbs, too. It sounds old-fashioned to invert the verb and subject with a pronoun such as *I* or *he*.

> *'What is it, little girl?'**he said**.*

> *'Bless her little heart!' **said he** with a big hug. (*old-fashioned – avoid this use)*

Reporting verbs and adverbs

Reporting verbs are often accompanied by extra information about the way something is said:

> *'And you won't go away?' I asked **gloomily**.*

> *Then he said – **very quietly indeed**, 'Open the door, my darling!'*

2 Look at the conversation that the story teller has with her husband at night, when she argues that the rest cure is not working. (Page 149). Answer the questions.

1 What reporting verbs does Perkins Gilman use, other than *say*?
2 How much of the conversation is reported a) directly, and b) indirectly?

3   Where do most of the reporting verbs come in the sentence? a) at the beginning, b) in the middle or c) at the end?

4   How many reporting verbs are inverted (i.e. the verb comes before the subject)?

3   Use the information above to convert this indirectly reported conversation between the story teller and her sister-in-law, Jennie, into direct speech. Use the sentence opening to help you start.

> *She didn't know I was in the room, and when I asked her in a quiet, a very quiet voice, with the most restrained manner possible, what she was doing with the paper – she turned around as if she had been caught stealing, and looked quite angry – asked me why I should frighten her so!*
>
> *Then she said that the paper stained everything it touched, that she had found yellow smooches on all my clothes and John's, and she wished we would be more careful!*

She didn't know I was in the room. 'What …

Vocabulary

Informal linking phrases

The story is written as a personal diary. One way that Perkins Gilman creates this effect is by using linking words that are normally used when speaking.

4   The meaning of sentences a) and b) is the same, but which would be more likely in an informal spoken situation?

I am getting angry enough to do something desperate. To jump out of the window would be admirable exercise, but the bars are too strong even to try.

*a) **Besides** I wouldn't do it. **It goes without saying**. I know well enough that a step like that is improper and might be misconstrued.*

*b) **What is more**, I wouldn't do it, **needless to say**. I know well enough that a step like that is improper and might be misconstrued.*

5   Match the informal linking phrases in bold with their uses and synonyms (a–h).

1   ***Still*** *I will proudly declare that there is something queer about it.*

2   ***Else**, why should it be let so cheaply?* (normally, '**or else**')

3   *There was some legal trouble, I believe, something about the heirs and coheirs;* **anyhow**, *the place has been empty for years.*

4   *I never thought of it before, but it is lucky that John kept me here after all, I can stand it so much easier than a baby,* **you see**.

5   *It is a dull yet lurid orange in some places, a sickly sulphur tint in others.* **No wonder** *the children hated it! I should hate it myself if I had to live in this room long.*

6   *And John is so queer now, that I don't want to irritate him. I wish he would take another room!* **Besides**, *I don't want anybody to get that woman out at night but myself.*

7   *John knows I don't sleep very well at night,* **for all** *I'm so quiet!*

8   **Why** *there's John at the door!*

a   used for saying that something remains true despite what you have just said or done (*nevertheless* ...)

b   used for saying that something must be true, because the situation would be different if it were not true (*otherwise* ...)

c   used when you are explaining something to check that the listener is following (*you understand*)

d   used for showing that you are not surprised by a particular situation or event (*unsurprisingly*...)

e   used for showing that you are surprised (*what an unexpected surprise!*)

f   used when you are adding another stronger reason to support what you are saying (*what is more*...)

g   used to say something happens in spite of something else (*in spite of the fact that*)

h   used when stating a particular fact which shows that something that has just been mentioned is not important (*anyway* ...)

6   This is another text that uses informal linking words. Put the text in order. The first and last sentences have been done.

a)   ... leave; he was so strict with me and never listened.
     Besides, ...

b)   ...the treatment wasn't right for me. And **no wonder**! ...   .

c)   Well, that's it, I've done it, I've left Mark. I can't quite believe it. Two nights ago I tried to creep out when he was asleep, but he woke up before I got to the door. But I was determined to keep trying, or else
     ...   ...*1*...

d)   ... I'm not sure what I'm going to do now.   ..*8*..

e) ... How can total separation from society help one feel more a part of society? **Anyhow,** ... .

f) ... how would I ever be happy? **You see,** I had to... ....

g) ... her shouting that I am being a fool. She could see that Mark never understood me. Yes, this is definitely for the best. **Still,** ...
....

h) ... last night I got out without him waking. I went straight to the railway station and am now at Sarah's house. I'm sure she secretly agrees that what I am doing is for the best **for all** ... .

Idiomatic expressions

7 Look at the idiomatic expressions from the story (1–8) and match them with their definitions (a–h).

1 out of spite
Explaining why she stripped the wallpaper off the wall:

*I told her that I did it **out of pure spite** at the vicious thing.*

2 on that score
After discussing the need to move with John:

*So of course I said no more **on that score**, and we went to sleep.*

3 take pains to do something
Describing her anger with John:

*But John says if I feel so, I shall neglect proper self-control; so I **take pains to** control myself ... and that makes me very tired.*

4 get the better of someone
John talking about the effect of the paper on his wife's mind:

*He said that I was letting it **get the better of me**.*

5 in/through the wars
Describing the damaged state of the furniture:

*this great heavy bed ... looks as if it had been **through the wars***

6 for (the) world/worlds
Expressing her relief that her child isn't in this room:

*Why, I wouldn't have a child of mine ... live in such a room **for worlds**.*

7 not hear of something
Discussing the possibility of moving to a different room:

*I wanted one downstairs ... but John **would not hear of it**.*

8 think straight

*It is getting to be a great effort for me to **think straight**.*

a used for emphasis, especially to show how much you would or would not do something
b used for referring to something that has just been mentioned
c to refuse to accept a suggestion or offer
d used to describe an action you do deliberately because you want to upset someone or cause problems for them
e *informal* to have injuries from being in an accident or fight
f *informal* to be able to see or think clearly
g to do something with a lot of care or effort
h used when an emotion or situation is too strong for you to control and it makes you do something that you did not intend to do

8 Match the sentence halves.

1 I said he could stay with us, but ...
2 He was too tired to be able to ...
3 He was angry with her and refused to come to the party ...
4 He had doubled sales, so his work had been a success ...
5 I had **taken great pains**...
6 Smith's anger **got the better of** him ...
7 Mike has **been in the wars**, look ...
8 He wouldn't sell his beloved golf clubs ...

a **on that score.**
b and he started to attack the referee.
c he's got a huge bruise on his face!
d **for the world.**
e **think straight.**
f **out of spite.**
g he **wouldn't hear of it**.
h to make the evening perfect.

Literary analysis

Plot

1 *The Yellow Wallpaper* does not contain a great deal of action, except towards the end. What are the main events leading up to the final scene?

2 The problem of communication between husband and wife is a serious concern in the story. The story teller says at one point:

It is so hard to talk with John about my case, because he is so wise, and because he loves me so.

Summarize in one sentence what the story teller believes would be a better way of treating her illness. What problems does she face when trying to explain this to John?

3 As the story progresses, we read signs that the story teller is losing touch with reality. Put these clues as to her disturbed mental state in the order in which they happened (1–10):

☐ She becomes suspicious of her husband's motives.

☐ She believes the woman in the wallpaper is real.

1 She begins to treat the wallpaper as an animate thing with a personality.

☐ She considers suicide.

10 She crawls over her unconscious husband.

☐ She gnaws the furniture.

☐ She identifies herself with the woman.

☐ She makes out a woman hidden in the pattern of the wallpaper.

☐ She sees the woman in the garden.

☐ She starts stripping the wallpaper.

4 Which of the signs in 3 do you find most disturbing? Why?

5 There are two aspects of the room that the story teller describes later in the story; they are the 'smooch', or streak, around the bottom of the wallpaper and the gnawed bedstead. Why do you think they are not mentioned until then? How do you account for their presence?

6 The story ends abruptly, with a disturbing scene of mental illness and desperation. What do you think happens after this, when John comes round from fainting? And later, what do you think the long-term effects of this episode are on:

a) the story teller's mental health
b) their relationship?
c) John's attitude to the rest cure?

7 Looking at your answers to a), b) and c) above, are you optimistic or pessimistic about the story teller's future?

Character

8 The story begins by describing the story teller and her husband as 'ordinary people'. What impression do you have of them? What sort of house and part of town do they normally live in? What sort of friends do they have?

9 What do the following extracts tell us about the story teller and her husband?

John laughs at me, of course, but one expects that in marriage.

If a physician of high standing, and one's own husband, assures friends and relatives that there is really nothing the matter with one but temporary nervous depression – a slight hysterical tendency – what is one to do?

10 There are certain basic facts we do not know about the main character. We are not even told her name. How old do you think she is? What does she look like? What does she wear? What sort of family does she come from? What does she like to do in her free time when she is not sick?

11 We do learn about the story teller from the things she writes about other than her illness, treatment and obsessions. How much does she say about the following things:
a) the house and garden
b) friends of theirs
c) their child
d) her husband's work
e) her writing
f) her duties as a wife

12 The wallpaper is not the only inanimate object that she talks about:

I never saw so much expression in an inanimate thing before, and we all know how much expression they have! I used to lie awake as a child and get more entertainment and terror out of blank walls and plain furniture than most children could find in a toy store.

I remember what a kindly wink the knobs of our big, old bureau used to have, and there was one chair that always seemed like a strong friend.

What does this tell us about her imagination? Is this a dangerous quality, as her husband believes? Why/Why not?

13 On the last day the story teller contemplates jumping out of the window but refuses to do it because she knows *'that a step like that is improper and might be misconstrued.'* What do you understand by that? What does it tell us about her?

14 What is your opinion of John? Do you sympathize with him in any way? Why?

Narration

15 The act of writing the story is an important element within the story; we read about the story teller's struggles as she tries to write:

I did write for a while in spite of them; but it does exhaust me a good deal – having to be so sly about it, or else meet with heavy opposition.

Find other moments in the story when she mentions writing. What prevents her from writing? Why does she write?

16 Notice how the flow of the narration is often interrupted for different reasons. Find examples of when the story teller …
a) has to stop writing because someone is coming.
b) changes subject very abruptly.

17 Which type of interruption reflects her disturbed state of mind? Which is used as a narrative device for moving the plot along?

18 There are occasional contradictions in what the story teller says. For example, she expresses relief that it is her staying in the nursery and not her child but then exclaims: 'I wish John would take me away from here!' What other contradictions do you notice in the story? What do they tell us about the story teller?

19 Think about how the story would have been told differently if it had been told by John. How would his diary have differed in style to his wife's? What would his concerns have been about her treatment? Her behaviour? The wallpaper? He is always telling her that she is improving; do you think that he really believes that? How would he have written about the last day?

20 What if the story teller had written it long after the events happened, not as a diary but as an autobiographical account? How would the story have been told differently then?

Style

21 The story is written in the form of a private diary. This allows
    Perkins Gilman to access her storyteller most secret thoughts,
    things that she would not dare tell anyone else. Here is an
    example:

    *John is a physician, and perhaps – (I would not say it to a living soul, of
    course, but this is dead paper and a great relief to my mind) – perhaps
    that is one reason I do not get well faster.*

    What information does the storyteller give here that she would not
    want to share with anyone else?

22 Read the extract then use the checklist below to note the elements
    the writer uses to give the effect of a personal diary:

    It makes me tired to follow it. I will take a nap I guess.

    I don't know why I should write this.

    I don't want to.

    I don't feel able.

    *And I know John would think it absurd. But I must say what I feel and
    think in some way – it is such a relief!*

    But the effort is getting to be greater than the relief.

    e.g. informal vocabulary ✓ *take a nap*
    ungrammatical sentences ✗
    diary entries stating the date
    a free, informal approach to punctuation
    a lack of normal paragraphing conventions
    a concern with personal issues
    signs that it is written in 'real time'
    crossings out, spelling errors and other signs that it has not been
    edited
    nicknames and abbreviations of common names, etc

23 Now read this extract. How is this unlike a diary? What effect is
    created?

    Why there's John at the door!

    It is no use, young man, you can't open it!

    How he does call and pound!

    Now he's crying for an axe.

    It would be a shame to break down that beautiful door!

24 The longest paragraph in the story is just a few lines, and most are just one sentence. Read out any section of the story with short paragraphs. What is the effect? How does the style reflect the story teller's personality and her state of mind?

25 Read this description of the wallpaper. Answer questions (a–e).

Looked at in one way each breadth stands alone, the bloated curves and flourishes – a kind of 'debased Romanesque' with delirium tremens – go waddling up and down in isolated columns of fatuity.

But, on the other hand, they connect diagonally, and the sprawling outlines run off in great slanting waves of optic horror, like a lot of wallowing seaweeds in full chase.

a) Are there any repeated words or phrases in her description?
b) How would you describe the vocabulary she uses here?
c) Look at the imagery she uses to describe the wallpaper; are the images similar or quite varied?
d) What is your impression of the wallpaper from her descriptions?
e) How does her style of writing reflect the wallpaper it is describing?

Simile and metaphor

26 A simile is a way of describing something by saying it is similar to something else. Similes are usually introduced with the word *like*. Perkins Gilman uses similes to build up a complicated description of the wallpaper.

Look at the extract in question 25 above. What is the paper being compared to?

27 Metaphor is when something is described by saying it *is* something else; the writer uses metaphors to develop the description further. Look at the metaphors in the extract below. What is the wallpaper being described as?

*You think you have mastered [the pattern], but just as you get well underway in following, **it turns a back-somersault** and there you are. **It slaps you in the face, knocks you down, and tramples upon you**.*

28 Look at the following extracts from the story. Which contain a) a simile, b) a metaphor, c) both?
a) There is a *delicious* garden!
b) One of those sprawling flamboyant patterns.
c) There is a recurrent spot where the pattern lolls like a broken neck and two bulbous eyes stare at you upside down.

d) I remember what a kindly wink the knobs of our big, old bureau used to have, and there was one chair that always seemed like a strong friend.

e) It is like a bad dream.

f) The outside pattern is a florid arabesque, reminding one of a fungus. If you can imagine a toadstool in joints, an interminable string of toadstools, budding and sprouting in endless convolutions – why, that is something like it.

g) The only thing I can think of that it is like is the *color* of the paper! A yellow smell.

29 Answer these questions:

a) Which images mix different senses?

b) Which images describe inanimate things as people?

c) Find a word other than *like* that is used to introduce a simile.

d) Which image do you find most disturbing? Why?

e) Which do you find most effective? Why?

Guidance to the above literary terms, answer keys to all the exercises and activities, plus a wealth of other reading-practice material, can be found at:
www.macmillanenglish.com/readers

The Lady or the Tiger?

by Frank R. Stockton

About the author

Frank R. Stockton, like Roald Dahl, was a well-known children's writer who delighted his adult readers as well. His light-hearted and often humorous view of life was reflected in all his stories, whether for adults or young readers. Unlike Dahl, many of his fairy tales for children, which in the late 19th century were hugely popular, have fallen out of fashion nowadays, but his intriguing story, *The Lady or the Tiger?*, is still widely read today.

Francis Richard Stockton was born in Philadelphia in the United States in 1834, one of nineteen children. His religious father didn't approve of fiction – he particularly hated novels – so while his father was still alive Francis kept his writing to a hobby. He specialized in fairy tales, a genre he had always loved since he was a child. When he grew up he did not go to college but worked as a wood engraver, an artist who illustrated books and magazines. He got married in 1860, the same year that his father died.

His first fairy tale to be published, *Ting-a-ling*, came out in 1867. More stories appeared in magazines for young people and in 1870 his first collection of short stories was published. He left the engraving business for a career in journalism. After working in New York on magazines for adults, he became assistant editor of a new magazine for children, *St. Nicholas* in 1873. It was for this magazine that his career as a children's writer really developed.

Unfortunately, he was forced to leave the magazine because of poor eyesight. He spent most of the rest of his writing career in a quiet suburb of New York, where he dictated his stories to a secretary from a hammock. Although he suffered from poor health, and couldn't walk very well, he was always excellent company, full of funny stories, and he left behind him many friends when he died in 1902.

Stockton sometimes drew his characters from life. His first commercial success, the novel *Rudder Grange*, is based on a girl Stockton hired to clean his house, and a humorous novel he wrote about two old ladies who are shipwrecked on a desert island is called *The Casting Away of Mrs. Lecks and Mrs. Aleshine*, women that the author knew.

However, many stories are set in impossible places full of fantastical creatures. One popular tale, *The Griffin and the Minor Canon*, is about a beast that is half eagle, half lion. The griffin comes to a village that has a statue of the same creature above the church door. Having never seen itself before, it becomes fascinated by its image, and stays. Its presence frightens the villagers, though, so they ask their priest to get rid of him. The griffin eats people, but only those it likes, and only twice a year. The problem is that he grows to like the priest, and so the animal is left with a dilemma, a difficult choice where neither option is satisfactory. We can see in this story the same playfulness with his readers that he shows in *The Lady or the Tiger?*. Both stories force us to think and decide the end of the story for ourselves.

About the story

The Lady or the Tiger? is Stockton's best-known short story. He wrote it for a local literary club of which he was a member, but it caused so much discussion during the club meeting that he decided to publish it in *The Century* magazine. When it appeared, in 1882, it captured the public imagination, much to Stockton's considerable surprise. People sent him letters asking him to clarify the ending, but he wisely refused to solve the puzzle for them. As Cleveland Moffett did for *The Mysterious Card*, Stockton wrote a sequel for the story, called *The Discourager of Hesitancy*, but this fails to throw any light on the mystery. Instead, it complicates matters by posing yet another impossible puzzle for the reader to think about.

The power of the story to generate discussion makes it a popular book to study at high school in America. In its day, it received attention from the famous British poet, Robert Browning, who wrote a poem about it, and a translation into Urdu allowed Hindu scholars to discuss it in great depth. More recently, it has been adapted for theatre, movie and television; an episode of *The Simpsons* refers to its ambiguous ending.

Background information

Barbarity versus civilization

The kingdom in which the story takes place is located far from its Latin neighbours, the Romans. In the 19th century, when the story was written, the Roman Empire was held in high regard as a model of civilization to copy and learn from. Civilizations that existed at the same time as the Romans were usually described negatively by historians as barbarian, cruel and uncivilized. Ancient peoples who were not Greek or Roman were even sometimes described as 'savage', which nowadays would be an insulting way of describing someone from a culture that is not considered technologically advanced. We now understand that although the Roman way of life was progressive in many ways, it was just as barbarian as many other cultures at the time.

The royal court

The society of the world in which the story is set is recognizably medieval, similar to the way that many countries used to be hundreds of years ago. The king is the absolute ruler, so much so that the country is defined as a kingdom belonging to him, and all the people who live there, his subjects, are subordinate to him. They look up to him without question.

Immediately around the king is the royal court; this is not just the place where he lives and works, it includes his family, servants, guards and advisors. The people that populate the court are known as courtiers, including young men hoping to impress the king and be given land as a reward for loyalty to him, and young maidens, unmarried women positioning themselves for a favourable marriage.

Ordinary people could only dream of entering the court; their position in life was far too low to be considered important enough.

The Roman arena

All of the action in the story takes place in an amphitheatre. An amphitheatre, or arena, was a large building, open to the sky, with many seats that rose up around the central area, which was used for public events such as sports competitions or plays. The Colosseum in Rome is the most famous amphitheatre in existence today. In the story, the architecture of the king's arena is borrowed from 'distant Latin neighbours', Latin being an adjective to describe the Romans.

The arena was designed to be extremely impressive, a sign of Rome's power. Large vaults, or arched ceilings, circled the building to shelter the people in the audience from the sun or the rain. They sat in balconies overlooking the action, also called galleries. The best seat in the amphitheatre was reserved for the most important person, sometimes the Emperor himself; he sat on a throne where he could see everyone and everyone could see him.

Roman amphitheatres were used for various forms of entertainment, but they weren't the sorts of shows that we are used to! Gladiators were armed men who fought animals, criminals and each other for sport. Another bloody spectacle popular in Roman times was watching Christians, who were persecuted for their religious opinions, being killed and eaten by lions. This is what is meant in the story by 'a conflict between religious opinions and hungry jaws'. The king in this story has a different use for his amphitheatre, but it is not much less bloody!

A fair judicial system

All human societies have laws and the means to judge law-breakers. The process of examining a case in a court of law and deciding whether someone is guilty or innocent is called a trial, or sometimes a tribunal. The fate of the accused person is normally decided by one person, a judge, or else a group of ordinary members of society. The perfect judge must show two key qualities. First, they must be impartial – they cannot be connected emotionally to either the criminal or the victim, nor can they be influenced in any way by either side. Second, they cannot be persuaded to do anything illegal or immoral, such as take money for a particular verdict. In other words, they must be incorruptible. If these qualities are present, then justice is more likely to be administered fairly, the truly innocent will go free and the guilty will be charged with the crime and face punishment.

Poetic justice

No real-life judicial system is perfect, of course, and is open to corruption and partiality; criminals go free. In literature, though, and in fairy tales in particular, it is often the case that the hero is rewarded and evil wrongdoers are punished at the end of the story. This is known as 'poetic justice'. Stockton calls his system an agent of poetic justice, and in many ways the system that you are going to read about in this story gets around the problems of partiality and corruptibility in a clever and simple way. You can decide for yourself whether it is fair.

Summary

It may help you to know something about what happens in the story before you read it. Don't worry, this summary does *not* tell you how the story ends!

The story is set in the far away land of a king who rules over his kingdom with absolute power. He alone decides all the laws and customs for his people. One strange but popular decision he has made is to turn criminal trials into public events held in the amphitheatre with the judgment being left to chance. He does this by having the accused person choose between two doors, one opening on to freedom and the chance of a new life, and the other bringing instant death.

The mechanism for this is surprisingly simple. Behind the first door stands a woman, chosen for the accused to be his wife, whether he likes it or not (it does not say what happens if the accused is a woman). If he chooses this door, he must marry her immediately; there is always a priest waiting to marry the couple and the couple are then free to leave. However, the other door hides a man-eating tiger, ready to jump out at him as soon as the door is opened. The audience enjoy the uncertainty of the event, celebrating the wedding if the accused is found innocent and crying if he is put to death.

The system seems to be working until one day the princess becomes involved. The trial takes on a new significance for the king because the accused man has been having a romance with his daughter, something he is not at all happy about. He allows the trial of chance to go ahead, knowing that either result will mean the young man can no longer be with the princess. The king ensures that the tiger is the fiercest, most dangerous animal in the whole kingdom, but he also makes certain that behind the other door is a lady beautiful enough for a man who dared to love a princess.

The day arrives, the audience assembles in the galleries of the amphitheatre and the man steps out into the arena. He alone must choose the door that will decide his fate: life or death. However, all is not lost. There may be someone who can help.

Pre-reading activities

Key vocabulary

This section will help you familiarize yourself with some of the more specific vocabulary used in the story. You may want to use it to help you before you start reading, or as a revision exercise after you have finished the story.

Displays of emotion

The people of the kingdom are very passionate and show their emotion easily.

1 **Decide which emotion (1–4) these extracts are describing.**

a) *Doleful iron bells were clanged, great **wails** went up from the hired **mourners**, and the vast audience, with **bowed** heads and downcast hearts, wended slowly their homeward way.*

b) *Then the **gay** brass bells rang forth their merry **peals**, the people shouted glad hurrahs. She had seen them walk away together upon their path of flowers, followed by the tremendous shouts of the **hilarious** multitude.*

c) *How in her **grievous** reveries had she **gnashed her teeth**, and torn her hair, she **shrieked** despairingly.*

d) *She imagined his start of **rapturous** delight as he opened the door of the lady, with her **flushing** cheek and sparkling eye.*

1 celebration
2 sadness
3 desire
4 frustration

2 **Check your answers with the definitions of the words in bold**

> **doleful** (adj) looking sad
> **wail** (n) a long, high shout or cry to show that you are in pain or are very sad
> **mourner** (n) someone who is at a funeral
> **bow** (v) to bend your head forwards so that you are looking down
> **gay** (adj) *old-fashioned* happy and excited
> **peal** (n) a sound of several bells ringing
> **hilarious** (adj) excited and cheerful
> **grievous** (adj) *formal* extremely serious or severe
> **gnash your teeth** (v) PHRASE to bite your teeth together and from side to side because you are very angry
> **shriek** (v) to shout in a loud high voice because you are frightened, excited, or surprised

> **rapturous** (adj) showing great happiness or excitement
> **flush** (v) if someone flushes, their face becomes red

3 **The adjectives in bold below describe intense emotions. Use the example sentences to help you understand their meaning, then match them with their definitions.**

*The United players were supported by an **exuberant** crowd, which may explain how they beat the favourites.*

*They had won the battle, but even the most **hot-blooded** soldiers among them knew they could do no more.*

*A mother made a **despairing** plea yesterday for a heart donor to save the life of her baby girl.*

*People were swept along with the crowd who filled the streets in **joyous** celebration of the great man's release.*

*I have always been one of his most **fervent** supporters.*

*The bride looked **radiant** as she walked down the aisle. The eyes of the whole church were on her.*

1 .... expressing great happiness
2 .... feeling that a situation is so bad that nothing you can do will change it
3 .... looking extremely happy
4 .... tending to have strong feelings, especially anger or sexual excitement
5 .... very enthusiastic and sincere, especially about something you believe in

4 **Answer the questions about the words studied in activities 1 to 3.**

1 Which word means the opposite of hopeful?
2 Which word means the opposite of radiant?
3 Which words convey the meaning of passionate love?
4 Which words are physical signs of emotion?
5 List the words associated with happiness.

Ways of thinking

The story is often held up as a popular example of a thought experiment for the reader, but there is a great deal of thinking within the story as well as around it.

5 **Read the extracts below and identify any words or phrases that describe ways of thinking and thought processes:**

> a) *There lived a semi-barbaric king, whose ideas, though somewhat polished and sharpened by the progressiveness of distant Latin neighbors, were still large, florid, and untrammeled.*
>
> b) *He was greatly given to self-communing, and, when he and himself agreed upon anything, the thing was done.*
>
> c) *It was in the public arena that the minds of his subjects were refined and cultured.*
>
> d) *She had possessed herself of the secret of the doors.*
>
> e) *The more we reflect upon this question, the harder it is to answer.*
>
> f) *Her decision had been indicated in an instant, but it had been made after days and nights of anguished deliberation.*
>
> g) *The question of her decision is one not to be lightly considered.*

6 **Now find these words and phrases in the extracts.**

1 a phrase which means to talk to yourself a lot
2 two adjectives which indicate that thoughts are not limited or controlled
3 three words that indicate careful thought
4 four verbs that mean to improve or civilize the thoughts or minds of uncultured people
5 a synonym for *gradual development* of ideas
6 a phrase synonymous with *find out* (information)

Formal words

Stockton writes with a rich and varied vocabulary, much of which is formal in style. He sometimes uses this formal tone to say things euphemistically. That is, to talk about unpleasant subjects without mentioning them.

7 The formal extracts (a–d) have informal equivalents in the sentences (1–4) following each one. Underline the formal words and phrases which correspond to the words and phrases in bold.

a) *He was a man of exuberant fancy, and, withal, of an authority so irresistible that, at his will, he turned his varied fancies into facts.*

He had a (1) **lively imagination**, and, (2) **what's more**, was (3) **so powerful** that he could make his dreams come true (4) **whenever he wanted**.

b) *When every member of his domestic and political systems moved smoothly in its appointed course, his nature was bland and genial; but, whenever there was a little hitch, and some of his orbs got out of their orbits, he was blander and more genial still, for nothing pleased him so much as to make the crooked straight and crush down uneven places.*

When everyone was doing their job (5) **as they should**, he was (6) **relaxed** and (7) **happy**, but whenever there was a (8) **problem** and people refused to do what they were told he was even more relaxed and happy, because nothing made him happier than to use his power to (9) **punish people**.

c) *Public notice was given that on an appointed day the fate of the accused person would be decided.*

(10) **There was an announcement** that on the (11) **set date** they would decide the future of the accused person.

d) *… although [the arena's] form and plan were borrowed from afar, its purpose emanated solely from the brain of this man.*

Although the king had borrowed his arena's design from (12) **a long way away**, it's use (13) **came** from his imagination (14) **alone**.

8 Match the words in bold in the extracts with their less formal equivalents in the box.

*He was (1) **subject to** no guidance or influence but that of the (2) **aforementioned** impartial and incorruptible chance.*

*It mattered not that his (3) **affections** might be engaged upon (4) **an object of his own selection**; the king allowed no such (5) **subordinate** arrangements to interfere with his great scheme.*

*He (6) **did not hesitate** nor waver in regard to his duty (7) **in the premises**.*

*Then such things were in (8) **no slight degree** (9) **novel** and startling.*

*Had it not been for the (10) **moiety of barbarism** in her nature it is probable that lady would not have been there, but her intense and (11) **fervid** soul would not allow her to (12) **be absent on** an occasion in which she was so terribly interested.*

cruel side	in the matter he faced	affected by
less important	miss	new quite	romantic feelings
someone he had chosen	that has already been mentioned
violent	wasted no time

Describing the princess

9 Read the definitions of adjectives that Stockton uses to describe the king's daughter. What impression do you have of her from them?

> **anguished** suffering great physical or emotional pain
> **blooming** looking healthy and attractive; often used about pregnant women
> **fervid** *formal* strong, violent, or extreme
> **imperious** behaving in a proud and confident way that shows you expect to be obeyed
> **semi-barbaric** (barbaric means violent and cruel)

Main themes

Before you read the story, you may want to think about some of its main themes. The questions will help you think about the story as you are reading it for the first time. There is more discussion of the main themes in the *Literary analysis* section after the story.

Barbarity versus civilization

The king in the story very much defines his own kingdom, and he is described as 'semi-barbaric', an uncultured, violent man whose ideas have been only slightly refined by the civilizing influence of the Romans. His daughter is described as similar to her father in this regard: she shares his 'savage blood'.

As you read the story, ask yourself:

a) How is the princess' love described in the story in terms of the opposing qualities of barbarity and civilization?

b) Does the barbaric culture of the princess have any bearing on her final decision?

Decision-making

The king's unusual system of justice replaces the important role of a judge or jury to make decisions about the guilt or innocence of a suspect with a lottery system that leaves the decision to chance. Even so, a significant proportion of the story is devoted to the theme of decision-making, and the powerful emotions that lie behind it.

As you read the story, ask yourself:

a) Who in the story makes decisions? What are they?
b) How seriously do the characters take the decisions? How do we know?
c) What roles do passion and jealousy have in the decision-making process?

⊘

The Lady or the Tiger?

by Frank R. Stockton

In the very olden time there lived a semi-barbaric king, whose ideas, though somewhat polished and sharpened by the **progressiveness** of distant Latin neighbors[1], were still large, florid, and untrammeled, as became the half of him which was barbaric. He was a man of exuberant fancy, and, withal, of an authority so **irresistible** that, at his will, he turned his varied fancies into facts. He was greatly given to self-communing, and, when he and himself agreed upon[2] anything, the thing was done. When every member of his domestic and political systems moved smoothly in its appointed course, his nature was bland and genial; but, whenever there was a little hitch, and some of his orbs[3] got out of their orbits, he was blander and more genial still, for nothing pleased him so much as to make the crooked straight and **crush** down uneven places.

Among the borrowed notions by which his barbarism had become semified[4] was that of the public arena, in which, by exhibitions of manly and beastly valor[5], the minds of his subjects were refined and cultured.

But even here the exuberant and barbaric fancy asserted itself. The arena of the king was built, not to give the people an opportunity of hearing the rhapsodies of dying gladiators, nor to enable them to view the inevitable conclusion of a conflict between religious opinions and hungry jaws, but for purposes far better adapted to widen and develop the mental energies of the people. This **vast** amphitheater, with its encircling galleries,

1 *American*: British English spelling *neighbour*
2 *formal* on
3 a reference to a metaphor of the people as 'orbs', bodies orbiting the king like the planets orbit the sun
4 an invented word, meaning to go from being fully barbaric to being half barbaric, or semi-barbaric
5 *formal*: the quality of being very brave, especially in war (*British spelling*: valour)

its mysterious vaults, and its unseen passages, was an agent of poetic justice, in which crime was punished, or virtue rewarded, by the decrees of an impartial and incorruptible chance.

When a subject was accused of a crime of sufficient importance to interest the king, public notice was given that on an appointed day the fate of the accused person would be decided in the king's arena, a structure which well deserved its name, for, although its form and plan were borrowed from afar, its purpose emanated solely from the brain of this man, who, every barleycorn[6] a king, knew no tradition to which he owed more allegiance than pleased his fancy, and who ingrafted[7] on every adopted form of human thought and action the rich growth of his barbaric idealism.

When all the people had assembled in the galleries, and the king, surrounded by his court, sat high up on his throne of royal state on one side of the arena, he gave a signal, a door beneath him opened, and the accused subject stepped out into the amphitheater. Directly opposite him, on the other side of the enclosed space, were two doors, exactly alike and side by side. It was the duty and the privilege of the person on trial to walk directly to these doors and open one of them. He could open either door he pleased; he was subject to no guidance or influence but that of the aforementioned impartial and incorruptible chance. If he opened the one, there came out of it a hungry tiger, the fiercest and most cruel that could be procured[8], which immediately sprang upon him and tore him to pieces as a punishment for his guilt. The moment that the case of the criminal was thus decided, doleful iron bells were clanged, great wails went up from the hired mourners posted on the outer rim of the arena, and the vast audience, with bowed heads and downcast hearts, wended[9] slowly their homeward

6 old-fashioned *phrase:* meaning 'every bit a king' (a barleycorn was an old unit of length equaling about 8mm)
7 *Biology:* to take a piece from a plant and join it to a cut made in another plant so that it can grow there
8 *formal:* to obtain something, especially with effort or difficulty
9 *literary:* if you wend your way somewhere, you go there

way, mourning greatly that one so young and fair, or so old and respected, should have merited so **dire** a fate.

But, if the accused person opened the other door, there came forth[10] from it a lady, the most suitable to his years and station that his majesty could select among his fair subjects, and to this lady he was immediately married, as a reward of his innocence. It mattered not that he might already possess a wife and family, or that his affections might be engaged upon an object of his own selection; the king allowed no such subordinate arrangements to interfere with his great scheme of retribution and reward. The exercises[11], as in the other instance, took place immediately, and in the arena. Another door opened beneath the king, and a priest, followed by a band of **choristers**, and dancing maidens blowing joyous airs[12] on golden horns and treading an epithalamic[13] measure, advanced to where the pair stood, side by side, and the wedding was promptly and cheerily solemnized. Then the gay brass bells rang forth their merry peals, the people shouted glad hurrahs, and the innocent man, preceded by children strewing flowers on his path, led his **bride** to his home.

This was the king's semi-barbaric method of administering justice. Its perfect fairness is obvious. The criminal could not know out of which door would come the lady; he opened either he pleased, without having the slightest idea whether, in the next instant, he was to be **devoured** or married. On some occasions the tiger came out of one door, and on some out of the other. The decisions of this tribunal were not only fair, they were positively determinate[14]: the accused person was instantly punished if he found himself guilty, and, if innocent, he was rewarded on the spot, whether he liked it or not. There was no escape from the judgments of the king's arena.

The institution was a very popular one. When the people gathered together on one of the great trial days, they never knew whether they were to witness a bloody **slaughter** or a hilarious

10 *literary:* away from a place; forwards, or out
11 *formal:* speeches and other ceremonial activities performed in front of an audience
12 *old-fashioned:* pieces of music that have a simple tune
13 *uncommon:* describing a song that celebrates marriage
14 *formal:* clearly fixed or decided

wedding. This element of uncertainty lent an interest to the occasion which it could not otherwise have attained[15]. Thus, the masses were entertained and pleased, and the thinking part of the community could bring no charge of unfairness against this plan, for did not the accused person have the whole matter in his own hands?

This semi-barbaric king had a daughter as blooming as his most **florid** fancies, and with a soul as fervent and imperious as his own. As is usual in such cases, she was **the apple of his eye**, and was loved by him above all humanity. Among his courtiers was a young man of that fineness of blood and lowness of station common to the conventional heroes of romance who love royal maidens. This royal maiden was well satisfied with her lover, for he was handsome and brave to a degree **unsurpassed** in all this kingdom, and she loved him with an ardor[16] that had enough of barbarism in it to make it exceedingly warm and strong. This love affair moved on happily for many months, until one day the king happened to discover its existence. He did not hesitate nor waver in regard to his duty in the premises. The youth was immediately cast into prison, and a day was appointed for his trial in the king's arena. This, of course, was an especially important occasion, and his majesty, as well as all the people, was greatly interested in the workings and development of this trial. Never before had such a case occurred; never before had a subject dared to love the daughter of the king. In after years such things became **commonplace** enough, but then they were in no slight degree novel and startling.

The tiger-cages of the kingdom were searched for the most savage and **relentless** beasts, from which the fiercest monster might be selected for the arena; and the ranks of maiden youth and beauty throughout the land were carefully surveyed by competent judges in order that the young man might have a **fitting** bride in case fate did not determine for him a different destiny. Of course, everybody knew that the deed with which the

15 *formal:* to succeed in achieving something, especially after a lot of effort
16 *literary:* very strong feelings of love (British spelling: ardour)

accused was charged had been done. He had loved the princess, and neither he, she, nor any one else, thought of denying the fact; but the king would not think of allowing any fact of this kind to interfere with the workings of the tribunal, in which he took such great delight and satisfaction. No matter how the affair turned out, the youth would be disposed of[17], and the king would take an **aesthetic** pleasure in watching the course of events, which would determine whether or not the young man had done wrong in allowing himself to love the princess.

The appointed day arrived. From far and near the people gathered, and **thronged** the great galleries of the arena, and crowds, unable to gain admittance, massed themselves against its outside walls. The king and his court were in their places, opposite the twin doors, those fateful portals[18], so terrible in their similarity.

All was ready. The signal was given. A door beneath the royal party opened, and the lover of the princess walked into the arena. Tall, beautiful, fair, his appearance was greeted with a low **hum** of admiration and anxiety. Half the audience had not known so grand a youth had lived among them. No wonder the princess loved him! What a terrible thing for him to be there!

As the youth advanced into the arena he turned, as the custom was, to bow to the king, but he did not think at all of that royal personage. His eyes were fixed upon the princess, who sat to the right of her father. Had it not been for the moiety[19] of barbarism in her nature it is probable that lady would not have been there, but her intense and fervid soul would not allow her to be absent on an occasion in which she was so terribly interested. From the moment that the **decree** had gone forth that her lover should decide his fate in the king's arena, she had thought of nothing, night or day, but this great event and the various subjects connected with it. Possessed of more power, influence, and force of character than any one who had ever before been interested in such a case, she had done what no

17 *formal:* to remove something such as a problem by dealing with it successfully
18 *literary:* doors; usually large, decorated entrances to a building
19 *formal:* uncommon: one of two parts of something

other person had done – she had possessed herself of the secret of the doors. She knew in which of the two rooms, that lay behind those doors, stood the cage of the tiger, with its open front, and in which waited the lady. Through these thick doors, heavily curtained with **skins** on the inside, it was impossible that any noise or suggestion should come from within to the person who should approach to raise the **latch** of one of them. But gold, and the power of a woman's will, had brought the secret to the princess.

And not only did she know in which room stood the lady ready to emerge, all **blushing** and radiant, should her door be opened, but she knew who the lady was. It was one of the fairest and loveliest of the damsels[20] of the court who had been selected as the reward of the accused youth, should he be proved innocent of the crime of aspiring to one so far above him; and the princess hated her. Often had she seen, or imagined that she had seen, this fair creature throwing **glances** of admiration upon the person of her lover, and sometimes she thought these glances were perceived, and even returned. Now and then she had seen them talking together; it was but for a moment or two, but much can be said in a brief space; it may have been on most unimportant topics, but how could she know that? The girl was lovely, but she had dared to raise her eyes to the loved one of the princess; and, with all the intensity of the savage blood transmitted to her through long lines of wholly barbaric ancestors, she hated the woman who blushed and **trembled** behind that silent door.

When her lover turned and looked at her, and his eye met hers as she sat there, paler and whiter than any one in the vast ocean of anxious faces about her, he saw, by that power of quick perception which is given to those whose souls are one, that she knew behind which door **crouched** the tiger, and behind which stood the lady. He had expected her to know it. He understood her nature, and his soul was assured that she would never rest until she had made plain to herself this thing, hidden

20 *old-fashioned:* a young woman who is not married

to all other lookers-on[21], even to the king. The only hope for the youth in which there was any element of certainty was based upon the success of the princess in discovering this mystery; and the moment he looked upon her, he saw she had succeeded, as in his soul he knew she would succeed.

Then it was that his quick and anxious glance asked the question: 'Which?' It was as plain to her as if he shouted it from where he stood. There was not an instant to be lost. The question was asked in a flash; it must be answered in another.

Her right arm lay on the cushioned parapet[22] before her. She raised her hand, and made a slight, quick movement toward the right. No one but her lover saw her. Every eye but his was fixed on the man in the arena.

He turned, and with a firm and rapid step he walked across the empty space. Every heart stopped beating, every breath was held, every eye was fixed immovably upon that man. Without the slightest hesitation, he went to the door on the right, and opened it.

Now, the point of the story is this: Did the tiger come out of that door, or did the lady?

The more we reflect upon this question, the harder it is to answer. It involves a study of the human heart which leads us through devious[23] mazes of passion, out of which it is difficult to find our way. Think of it, fair reader, not as if the decision of the question depended upon yourself, but upon that hot-blooded, semi-barbaric princess, her soul at a white heat beneath the combined fires of despair and jealousy. She had lost him, but who should have him?

How often, in her waking hours and in her dreams, had she started in wild horror, and covered her face with her hands as she thought of her lover opening the door on the other side of which waited the cruel fangs of the tiger!

21 *uncommon:* someone who watches something happen but does not take part in it (normally 'onlookers')
22 *architecture:* a low wall
23 *formal:* not direct

But how much oftener had she seen him at the other door! How in her grievous reveries[24] had she gnashed her teeth, and torn her hair, when she saw his start of rapturous delight as he opened the door of the lady! How her soul had burned in agony when she had seen him rush to meet that woman, with her flushing cheek and sparkling eye of triumph; when she had seen him lead her forth, his whole frame kindled[25] with the joy of recovered life; when she had heard the glad shouts from the multitude, and the wild ringing of the happy bells; when she had seen the priest, with his joyous followers, advance to the couple, and make them man and wife before her very eyes; and when she had seen them walk away together upon their path of flowers, followed by the tremendous shouts of the hilarious multitude, in which her one despairing shriek was lost and drowned!

Would it not be better for him to die at once, and go to wait for her in the blessed regions of semi-barbaric futurity[26]?

And yet, that awful tiger, those shrieks, that blood!

Her decision had been indicated in an instant, but it had been made after days and nights of anguished deliberation. She had known she would be asked, she had decided what she would answer, and, without the slightest hesitation, she had moved her hand to the right.

The question of her decision is one not to be lightly considered, and it is not for me to presume to set myself up as the one person able to answer it. And so I leave it with all of you: Which came out of the opened door – the lady, or the tiger?

24 *literary:* thoughts that make you forget what you are doing or what is happening around you
25 *literary:* if an emotion kindles, it begins to develop
26 *formal:* future time

Post-reading activities

Understanding the story

Use these questions to check that you have understood the story.

The king and his arena

1 Why is the king described as only semi-barbaric?
2 Whose advice does he ask for when making decisions about government?
3 How is the king's amphitheatre similar to Roman ones? How is it different?
4 Draw a diagram of the amphitheatre. Label it with the following features: galleries, doors, throne, seating for the court, seating for the general public.

The workings of the trial

5 If the outcome of a trial is a guilty verdict, what is the punishment? When is the punishment carried out?
6 What if the verdict is innocent? What is the reward? Why is this not always desirable?
7 How does Stockton justify as 'fair' the justice system described in the story?
8 Why is a trial in the arena such a popular event?

The case of the princess and her lover

9 How did the princess know the young man?
10 What makes him a suitable candidate to be the princess' partner? What makes him unsuitable?
11 Why did their relationship end?
12 What evidence is there to suggest that the king is more interested in this trial than in other trials? Why is this?
13 What evidence is there to suggest that the general public is more interested in this trial than in other trials?
14 What impression does the audience have of the young man?
15 What information has the princess managed to discover?
16 How did she manage to find out these secrets?
17 Why is the choice of lady that has been made for the trial particularly difficult for the princess to accept?
18 What information does the young man gather from his quick look at the princess?
19 How is it possible for the young man to understand this in one momentary look?
20 Which door does the young man choose? Why?

21 How has the princess been feeling about the two possible outcomes of the trial?

22 How long did it take her to decide which door to point him to?

23 What do you think: did the tiger come out of that door, or did the lady?

Language study

Grammar

Prepositions in relative clauses

In everyday modern usage when we use prepositions with a relative pronoun (*which, who, that*) the preposition comes at the end of the clause. If, in your first language, prepositions don't normally go at the end of clauses, this may seem strange to you.

> The door **which** the lady would come **out of**.

> The tiger **that** he had nightmares **about**.

Notice that Stockton puts prepositions before the pronoun.

> This man knew no tradition **to which** he owed more allegiance than pleased his fancy.

> Everybody knew that the deed **with which** the accused was charged had been done.

> Her soul would not allow her to be absent on an occasion **in which** she was so terribly interested.

This structure is formal, and usually only found in formal written texts. It can make a text sound old-fashioned if it is used too much.

When the relative pronoun refers to a person, *who* or *whom* is used depending on whether the person is the subject or the object of the relative clause:

> The princess **who** thought **about** him constantly while he was in prison.

> The princess **whom** he thought **about** constantly while he was in prison.

Whom is rather old-fashioned nowadays and can be replaced by *who*.

> The princess **who** he thought **about** constantly while he was in prison.

However, if the preposition goes before the relative pronoun, *whom* is always used:

> The princess **about whom** he thought constantly while he was in prison.

1 **Combine the two sentences. Use a relative pronoun and the preposition in bold. In an informal sentence, put the preposition at the end of the clause. In a formal sentence put it before the relative pronoun.**

e.g. There was a large amphitheatre in the town. Criminals were put on trial **in** the amphitheatre. (formal)

There was a large amphitheatre in the town in which criminals were put on trial.

1 The king had a daughter. He was very proud **of** her. (informal)
   The king

2 The man had been accused **of** a crime. Everybody knew that he had committed the crime. (formal)
   Everybody knew

3 The amphitheatre was the tallest building in the city. Everybody was walking **towards** it. (formal)
   The amphitheatre,

4 He looked at the woman. He had fallen in love **with** her. (informal)
   He looked

5 He stood **before** the two doors. He did not hesitate to choose between them. (formal)
   He did

Dummy *there*

Fairy tales tend to begin in very similar ways, typically:

   Once upon a time there was a beautiful princess /wicked queen / etc …

The Lady or the Tiger? establishes itself as a fairy tale from the first line of the story. It introduces a main character with *there* + past verb:

   *In the very olden time **there lived** a semi-barbaric king …*

Notice that the sentence could be expressed differently, without *there*:

   *In the very olden time a semi-barbaric king **lived** …*

There is a dummy pronoun, which is used to make a statement about the existence of something; 'There was a king' means 'A king existed'. Although its use with the verb *to be* is very familiar to us, its use with *lived* and other verbs is more unusual. It exists in a few fixed expressions:

   There comes *a time in everyone's life when a big decision has to be taken.*

Normally, however, its use with verbs other than *to be* is restricted to literature. It sounds old-fashioned, which is why Stockton uses it in this fairy tale.

There has other uses, of course, most commonly as an adverbial to mean 'in that place':

> *What a terrible thing for him to be **there**!*

2 **Notice the use of *there* in the following extracts. Which one is *not* a dummy pronoun?**

a) *Whenever there was a little hitch, he was blander and more genial still.*

b) *If he opened the one, there came out of it a hungry tiger*

c) *There was no escape from the judgments of the king's arena.*

d) *Had it not been for the moiety of barbarism in her nature it is probable that lady would not have been there*

Look at sentence a) again. To express the sentence without *there*, another word would need to be added:

> *Whenever a little hitch **occurred**, he was blander and more genial still.*

3 **Rewrite sentences b) and c) without using *there*. Which sentence does not need any extra words added? Why?**

Multiple-clause sentences

One of the features of an authentic text is a variety in sentence length. Some of the sentences in the story are quite short – only a few words. They are often used to create a dramatic effect:

> *All was ready. The signal was given.*

> *There was not an instant to be lost.*

Other sentences contain many clauses, so their structure is often very complex. They may be used to set the scene, create atmosphere, change the pace or to sum up a situation because they can condense a lot of details into one sentence. Look at this example. The clauses are numbered:

> *(1) The only hope for the youth (2) in which there was any element of certainty (3) was based upon the success of the princess in discovering this mystery; and (4) the moment he looked upon her, (5) he saw she had succeeded, as (6) in his soul he knew she would succeed.*

Look at how the clauses break down into short sentences.

1 There was one hope for the young man.

2 It was the only certain hope he had.
3 It was based on the princess succeeding in discovering the truth.
4 He looked at her.
5 He saw that she had succeeded.
6 He had always known that she would succeed.

In this case, the long sentence helps to convey the thought process of the young man as he reasons optimistically for his lover to help him.

4 **Look at another example. How many clauses are there in the sentence? Use commas to separate the clauses where necessary. Check your answers on page 184.**

When all the people had assembled in the galleries and the king surrounded by his court sat high up on his throne of royal state on one side of the arena he gave a signal a door beneath him opened and the accused subject stepped out into the amphitheater.

5 **Now break the sentence down into separate sentences. Compare your sentences to the one in the story. What is the difference in the effect?**

You will find examples of multiple-clause sentences throughout your reading of authentic texts. They can be very effective but their length and complexity can also be confusing. If you find multiple-clause sentences difficult, break them down into shorter clauses as you have done here – this may make it easier to understand.

Literary analysis

Plot

1 What are the main events in the story? Over how long do the events of the story take place?
2 What are the princess' reasons for choosing the lady? What reasons does she have for choosing the tiger?
3 Imagine you are directing a movie of the story. Think about the final moments in the amphitheatre. How would you direct the scene? Ask yourself the following questions:
   a) What will your first shot be to set the scene?
   b) What is the atmosphere in the arena? How will you create mood?
   c) What do the doors look like?
   d) How are the king and princess dressed? And the people?
   e) What are the king and the princess doing before the young man is sent into the arena?

f) What are the expressions on the faces of the king, the princess, the young man and the audience when the man enters?

g) How should the princess communicate to her lover which door to choose without being observed by anyone in the arena?

h) What is the final shot of the movie?

4   Write the words to a 30-second 'trailer', or advert, for your film.

5   What does the story tell us about passion and jealousy?

6   The story could be seen as a type of fairy tale, even though Stockton's intended readers were not children, or not only children, at any rate. What elements of a fairy tale do you notice in the story? In which ways is it not a fairy tale?

Character

7   In what order are the characters introduced? Why?

8   Throughout the story there is no speech and little physical description of the characters. How does Stockton tell us what they are like? What do we learn about them?

9   Who do we learn the most about? Why is this?

10 The young man's character is described as 'common to the conventional heroes of romance'. In what ways is he a typical hero?

11 What about the king? Is there anything conventional about him? And the princess? Is she a stereotype of a fairytale princess in any way?

12 What aspects of the princess' character would affect her decision in the arena? How would they affect it?

13 Why is it important that the princess is similar to her father?

14 If you were the young man would you choose the door on the right or the left? Is he right to trust his lover?

15 Do you sympathize with any of the characters? Are we supposed to sympathize with the characters in this story?

Narration

16 How much of the story is a narration of events? In other words, what percentage of the story tells what happens?

17 Stockton organizes the story clearly. Put the topics in the order in which they appear.

a) An outline of the princess' affair with the young man, its discovery by the king and the beginning of the judicial process.

b) An introduction to the other main characters.

c) A description of the beginning of the young man's trial.

d) A justification for the judicial system.

e) A description of the final moments of the trial.

f) A description of the king's absolute rule.

g) An introduction to the public arena and its purpose.

h) A study of the princess' conflicting motivations.

i) An explanation of the princess' secret investigation before the trial.

j) The details of the punishment and reward.

k) The procedure of a typical trial.

18 The story teller frequently addresses his readers directly, as he does at the very end of the story:

> ... it is not for me to presume to set myself up as the one person able to answer it. And so I leave it with all of you: Which came out of the opened door – the lady, or the tiger?

He tries to balance the opposing arguments for the princess to choose one door over the other. Do you think that he succeeds in showing no partiality of his own, or do you sense a preference for one verdict? If so, why is that?

19 What is the purpose of the last seven paragraphs of the story? Do you think they are necessary?

Style

Fairytale English

Stockton's style in *The Lady or the Tiger?* can be described as formal and old-fashioned. Certain elements of his style are suitable for telling a tale or legend set in an imaginary past. For example, when Stockton is describing the princess' secret investigations, he inverts, or changes the order of, the subject and the verb:

> She knew in which of the two rooms **stood the cage of the tiger**, and in which **waited the lady**.

Standard modern English would express this as: '... *the cage of the tiger stood.* ... *the lady waited*'

20 Read the extract. Then match the examples from the extract with the different elements of formal, old-fashioned style.

> But, if the accused person opened the other door, there came forth from it a lady, the most suitable to his years and station that his majesty could select among his fair subjects, and to this lady he was immediately married, as a reward of his innocence. It mattered not that he might already possess a wife and family …

It mattered not…
… there came forth from it a lady.
… to this lady he was immediately married.

a) inversion of the subject and verb for a poetic effect
b) inversion of the object and the subject
c) an omission of the auxiliary 'did' to make a negative

21 What formal, old-fashioned vocabulary can you see in the extract that adds to the overall fairytale style?

The use of questions

The story is, of course, famous for its final question; it is so central to the story that Stockton made the question the title. Usually, questions are meant to be answered, of course; when the young man looks to his lover in the arena and, with his eyes, asks 'Which?', there is a quick and immediate response from the princess.

There are questions that don't require an answer; these are called 'rhetorical questions' and they may be used for a variety of reasons:

a) to criticize:

'You took my car without asking! What were you thinking?!'

b) to convince the listener, or oneself, of a point of view that may be difficult to justify:

'Can't a man borrow a friend's car for a couple of hours?'

c) to express a difficult decision that does not seem to have an answer:

'The car's been stolen. How am I going to tell him?'

d) to state the obvious:

'You think I should tell him the truth … Do I look stupid?'

22 Look at the extracts. Why does Stockton ask these questions? Choose one of reasons (a–d) above:

About the trial system:

Did not the accused person have the whole matter in his own hands?

About the princess' reasons for jealousy:

Now and then she had seen them talking together; it may have been on most unimportant topics, but how could she know that?

The princess debating which door to indicate:

She had lost him, but who should have him?

Would it not be better for him to die at once, and go to wait for her in the blessed regions of semi-barbaric futurity?

Long exclamations

An exclamation is a sentence that expresses strong emotion such as anger, surprise or joy. Usually, exclamations are very short, and they may not show the usual structure of a sentence:

Oi!   Urgh!   How wonderful!   Oh my goodness!

Stockton uses longer exclamations in his description of the thought processes of the princess.

23   Read the extract below. How many of the sentences are exclamations? What effect do they have?

How often, in her waking hours and in her dreams, had she started in wild horror, and covered her face with her hands as she thought of her lover opening the door on the other side of which waited the cruel fangs of the tiger!

But how much oftener had she seen him at the other door! How in her grievous reveries had she gnashed her teeth, and torn her hair, when she saw his start of rapturous delight as he opened the door of the lady! How her soul had burned in agony when she had seen him rush to meet that woman, with her flushing cheek and sparkling eye of triumph; when she had seen him lead her forth, his whole frame kindled with the joy of recovered life; when she had heard the glad shouts from the multitude, and the wild ringing of the happy bells; when she had seen the priest, with his joyous followers, advance to the couple, and make them man and wife before her very eyes; and when she had seen them walk away together upon their path of flowers, followed by the tremendous shouts of the hilarious multitude, in which her one despairing shriek was lost and drowned!

Guidance to the above literary terms, answer keys to all the exercises and activities, plus a wealth of other reading-practice material, can be found at: www.macmillanenglish.com/readers.

Essay questions

Language analysis

Discuss how **one** of the language areas you have studied contributes to the telling of two (or more) of the stories in the collection.

Analysing the question

What is the question asking?

It is asking you to:

- choose one language area from the index on page 207
- explain how this language area functions in the context of storytelling
- use examples from two (or more) of the stories in the collection.

Preparing your answer

1 Look back through the *Language study* sections of the stories you've read and choose a language area that you feel confident about and that applies to the telling of two, or more, of the stories.
2 Make notes about the language area. Include notes on form, function and use.
3 Choose examples from two, or more stories.
4 Look back at the question and your notes and plan your essay. Here is an example of an essay plan:

Introduction	Introduce the area you are going to talk about.
Main body 1	Explain the general function of the area you have chosen. Use examples from more than one story.
Main body 2	Analyse how the area contributes to the style and atmosphere of the stories, referring to specific passages in the stories.
Conclusion	Summarize the literary use and function of the language area you focused on.

Literary analysis

Choose two of the stories in the collection. Compare and contrast the nature of the mystery that they describe, how the mystery is portrayed and the differences and similarities between them.

Analysing the question

What is the question asking?

It is asking you to:
- look at two stories in the collection
- outline the nature of the mystery that they describe
- explain how the mystery is described
- describe any similarities and differences

Preparing your answer

1 Choose two stories whose mysteries interest you and that are different enough to allow you to contrast them.
2 Make notes about the nature of the mystery: what makes the story mysterious and how the writer generates a sense of mystery.
3 Find key scenes in the stories where the mysteries are described or the atmosphere created. Make a note of any useful quotations.
4 Make a list of similarities and differences between the stories in regard to the mystery in each one; think of the story teller's attitude to the mystery, whether the story resolves the mystery in any way, how realistic the story is and your own reaction to the mystery.
5 Read the question again and write a plan for your essay. Here is an example:

Introduction	Briefly introduce the two stories.
Main body 1	Describe the two stories in terms of the mysteries in them.
Main body 2	Discuss the ways that the two writers create a sense of mystery and how each mystery is described.
Main body 3	Describe what the two stories have in common with regard to mystery and how they differ.
Conclusion	Make a general comment about mystery as described in these mystery stories.

Glossary

The definitions in the glossary refer to the meanings of the words and phrases as they are used in the short stories in this collection. Some words and phrases may also have other meanings which are not given here. The definitions are arranged in the story in which they appear, and in alphabetical order.

The Lost Special

acute (adj) if someone has an acute sense or ability, they notice things very quickly and easily

ally (n) someone who is ready to help you, especially against someone else who is causing problems for you

ample (adj) enough, and often more than you need

annals (plural n) the official records of an organization, arranged according to their date

appalled (adj) offended or shocked very much by something, because it is extremely unpleasant or bad

at stake PHRASE likely to be lost or damaged if something fails

bait (n) someone who is used for attracting and catching someone else, especially a criminal

bear a resemblance (past *bore*) | PHRASE if you bear a resemblance to someone, you look like them

beckon (v) *literary*: to signal to someone to come towards you

boast (v) to proudly tell other people about what you have done or can do, especially in order to make them admire you

coroner (n) someone whose job is to decide officially how a person died, especially if they died in a sudden or violent way

deed (n) something that someone does

farce (n) a situation or event that is silly because it is very badly organized, unsuccessful, or unfair

flaw (n) a mark or fault that spoils something and makes it less beautiful or perfect

formidable (adj) very impressive in size, power, or skill and therefore deserving respect and often difficult to deal with

grimly (adv) in a very serious and unfriendly way

grotesque (adj) extremely strange, ugly and unreasonable

hand (n) someone who does physical work, especially on a farm or a ship

hoax (n) a trick in which someone deliberately tells people that something bad is going to happen or that something is true when it is not

imposing (adj) large and impressive

in the throes PHRASE if you are in the throes of something you are involved in a difficult or unpleasant situation or activity

inquest (n) an official attempt by a court to find the cause of someone's death

jolting (n) a sudden violent movement

libel (n) the illegal act of writing things about someone that are not true

mischief (n) trouble or disagreement that someone deliberately causes

moorings (n) from the verb, *moor*, to stop a ship or boat from moving by fastening it to a place with ropes or by using an anchor

oath (n) a formal promise, especially one made in a court of law

obstinate (adj) not willing to be reasonable and change your plans, ideas, or behaviour

pawnbroker (n) someone whose job is to lend money to people in exchange for a valuable object that they can sell if the person does not return the money

preposterous (adj) extremely unreasonable or silly

puny (adj) small, thin and weak

quay (n) a hard surface next to a sea or river, where boats can stop

reprieve (n) an official decision not to kill someone who was going to be killed as a punishment

shaft (n) a long narrow passage, for example one that leads from the surface of the ground down to a mine

slaughter house (n) a building where animals are killed for their meat

stoop (n) a way of standing or walking with your head and shoulders bent forwards and downwards

subtle (adj) not obvious, and therefore difficult to notice

trace (n) a slight sign that someone has been present or that something has happened

undertaking (n) something difficult or complicated that you do

unprecedented (adj) never having happened or existed before

wield (v) to have and be able to use power or influence

The Mysterious Card

cease (v) to stop doing something

conjure up PHRASAL VERB to bring something such as a feeling or memory to your mind

consequential (adj) *formal*: important

decipher (v) to succeed in understanding the meaning of something written in a code

fatal (adj) with very serious negative effects

fellow (n) *old-fashioned*: a man

flimsy (adj) not easy to believe

gesticulate (v) to make movements with your hands and arms when you are talking

ill-fated (adj) *mainly journalism*: likely to end in failure or death

infernal (adj) used for emphasizing how annoying or unpleasant something is

jolly (adj) *old-fashioned*: lively and enjoyable

non-committal (adj) not saying what you think or what you plan to do

quarters (n) *formal*: rooms or buildings for people to live in

riddle (n) something that is mysterious or confusing

row (n) *old-fashioned*: a lot of noisy activity

rugged (adj) strong and able to deal with difficult conditions

scrawl (n) untidy, careless writing

sprawling (adj) stretching across something in an ugly and untidy way

vestige (n) a very small amount of something

wharf (n) a structure built for boats to stop at, at the edge of the land or leading from the land out into the water

yield (v) *formal*: to finally agree to do what someone else wants you to do

The Mildenhall Treasure

adjourn (v) to temporarily end something such as a meeting or a trial

array (n) a large group of people or things that are related in some way

bitter (adj) extremely cold in a way that makes you very uncomfortable

bitterness (n) a feeling of anger because of a bad experience, especially when you think you have been treated unfairly

conceal (v) *formal*: to hide something so that it cannot be found

crumbly (adj) breaking easily into very small pieces

crust (n) a hard layer of a substance

cultivated (adj) cultivated land is used for growing crops or plants

enthralling (adj) so interesting or exciting that you give it all your attention

far and away PHRASE used for saying that something has much more of a particular quality than anything else

flecked (adj) with small spots of colour

the game's up PHRASE used for saying that the truth has been discovered, especially when someone has been doing something wrong and will have to stop

glint (n) a quick flash of light

hang on to PHRASAL VERB *informal*: to keep something

jerk (n) a quick sudden movement

jolt (n, v) a sudden violent movement

jumpy *informal*: nervous

kick yourself PHRASE to be very annoyed because you have made a mistake, missed an opportunity etc

kneel down PHRASAL VERB to put one or both knees on the ground

liquidate (v) *informal*: to kill someone

lodge (v) to become firmly fixed somewhere, usually accidentally

lukewarm (adj) not hot or cold enough to be enjoyable

malice (n) a strong feeling of wanting to hurt someone or be unkind to them

mania (n) a mental illness that makes someone behave in an extremely excited and active way

pounce (v) to quickly jump on or hold someone or something

premonition (n) a strong feeling that something is going to happen, especially something bad

prosperous (adj) rich and successful

rim (n) the edge of an open container or circular object

rust (n) the rough red substance that damages the surface of iron and steel

sack (n) a large strong bag for storing and carrying things

shattered (adj) extremely upset

shiver (n) a shaking movement that your body makes when you are cold, frightened, or excited

sideboard (n) a large piece of furniture that has shelves and cupboards for storing dishes, glasses etc

skimp (v) to not spend enough time or money on something

sound (adj) safe or in good condition

sour (adj) unpleasant, unfriendly, or in a bad mood

spade (n) a tool used for digging that consists of a handle and a flat metal part that you push into the earth with your foot

splutter (v) *informal*: to make noises with your mouth because you suddenly cannot breathe or swallow normally

stooped (v) to bend the top half of your body downwards

stubble (n) the ends of plants that are left above ground after a farmer cuts a crop such as wheat or barley

stuff (n) *informal*: a variety of objects or things

superfluous (adj) not needed or wanted

testify (v) to provide evidence that something exists or is true

tipsy (adj) *informal*: slightly drunk

vital (adj) very important, necessary, or essential

The Yellow Wallpaper

astonish (v) to surprise someone very much

axe (n) a tool used for cutting down trees and cutting up large pieces of wood, consisting of a long wooden handle and a heavy metal blade

bulbous (adj) big and round

check (v) to stop yourself or someone else from doing something

conspicuous (adj) very noticeable or easy to see, especially because of being unusual or different

earnest (adj) serious, determined, and meaning what you say

faint (v) to suddenly become unconscious for a short time, and usually fall to the ground

flourish (v) to grow well and be healthy

fretful (adj) worried and unhappy, especially because of being nervous or tired

gloomily, (adv) in a way that shows you are feeling sad and without hope

gnarly, gnarled (adj) old and twisted and covered in lines

gnaw (v) to keep biting something

hug (n) the action of putting your arms round someone to show your love or friendship

improper (adj) not suitable or right according to accepted standards of social or professional behaviour

knob (n) a round handle on a door or drawer

lease (n) a legal contract in which you agree to pay to use someone else's building, land, or equipment for a specific period of time

let something or someone alone PHRASE if you let something alone, you do not touch it or do anything to it; if you let someone alone, you don't disturb or annoy them

mansion (n) a large house, especially a beautiful one

nap (n) *informal*: a short sleep, usually during the day

out of spite PHRASE if you do something out of spite, you do it because you want to upset someone, especially because you think something is unfair

outrageous (adj) extremely unusual and likely to shock people

peel off PHRASAL VERB to remove something from the surface of something else, especially by taking one end or side and pulling it up

plaster (n) a substance that is spread onto walls and ceilings to form a hard smooth surface

pound (v) to hit something several times with a lot of force

rare (adj) rare meat has been cooked for only a short time and is red inside

ravages (plural n) the damage or destruction caused by something such as war, disease, or extreme weather

recurrent (adj) happening again, especially several times

scoff (v) to laugh or say things to show that you think someone or something is stupid or deserves no respect

see through someone PHRASAL VERB to realize what someone is really like or what they are really doing and not be tricked by them

seldom (adv) not often

shade (n) a particular form of a colour. For example sky blue and navy blue are shades of blue.

shady, shaded (adj) hidden from the sun or other light

sly (adj) clever at tricking people or at doing things secretly

smoulder (v) to burn slowly, producing smoke but no flames

subdued (adj) quiet and slightly sad or worried

untenanted (adj) if a house is untenanted, no one lives there

wharf (n) a structure built for boats to stop at, at the edge of the water

wink (n and v) the action of quickly closing and opening one eye as a sign to someone

worthwhile (adj) if something is worthwhile, it is worth the time, money, or effort that you spend on it

The Lady or the Tiger?

aesthetic (adj) relating to beauty or to the study of the principles of beauty, especially in art

the apple of someone's eye PHRASE the person that someone loves most of all and is very proud of

blush (v) if you blush, your cheeks become red because you feel embarrassed or ashamed

bride (n) a woman who is getting married, or who has recently married

chorister (n) member of a choir (= a group of people singing together)

commonplace (adj) not unusual

crouch (v) to move your body close to the ground by bending your knees and leaning forwards slightly

crush (v) to hit or press something so hard that you damage it severely or destroy it, especially by making its shape flatter

decree (n) an official decision or order made by a leader or government

devour (v) to eat something very fast because you are hungry

dire (adj) very severe or serious

fitting (adj) suitable for a particular situation

florid (adj) containing too much decoration

glance (n) a quick look at someone or something

hum (n) a low continuous sound made by a machine or a lot of people talking

irresistible (adj) strong or powerful and impossible to control or defeat

latch (n) an object for keeping a door, gate etc fastened shut, consisting of a metal bar that fits into a hole or slot

progressive (adj) supporting social and political change that aims to make a system fairer; **progressiveness** (n)

relentless (adj) determined, and never stopping your attempts to achieve something

skin (n) the outer layer cut from an animal's body, used for making clothing and decorations

slaughter (n) the violent killing of a person or animal

throng (v) if people throng somewhere, a lot of them go there

tremble (v) if your body or part of your body trembles, it shakes, usually because you are nervous, afraid, or excited

unsurpassed (adj) better than everything or everyone else in a particular way

vast (adj) extremely large

Dictionary extracts adapted from the *Macmillan English Dictionary 2nd Edition* © Macmillan Publishers Limited 2007 www.macmillandictionary.com

Language study index

The Lost Special

Speculating about the past – past modal verbs
Subjunctive use of *should*
Metaphorical language – understanding is seeing

The Mysterious Card

Participle clauses
No sooner, *scarcely* and *just* for dramatic narrative
Use of epithets

The Mildenhall Treasure

Inversion in conditional sentences
Fronting in informal speech
Phrasal verbs with *up*

The Yellow Wallpaper

I wish and *if only*
Reporting direct speech
Informal linking phrases
Idiomatic expressions

The Lady or the Tiger?

Prepositions in relative clauses
Dummy *there*
Multiple-clause sentences

Visit the Macmillan Readers website at
www.macmillanenglish.com/readers

to find FREE resources for use in class and for independent learning. Search our online catalogue to buy new Readers including audio download and eBook versions.

Here's a taste of what's available:

For the classroom:

- **Tests** for every Reader to check understanding and monitor progress
- **Worksheets** for every Reader to explore language and themes
- **Listening worksheets** to practise extensive listening
- Worksheets to help prepare for the **FCE reading exam**

Additional resources for students and independent learners:

- An **online level test** to identify reading level
- **Author information sheets** to provide in-depth biographical information about our Readers authors
- **Self-study worksheets** to help track and record your reading which can be used with any Reader
- Use our **creative writing worksheets** to help you write short stories, poetry and biographies
- Write academic essays and literary criticism confidently with the help of our **academic writing worksheets**
- Have fun completing our **webquests** and **projects** and learn more about the Reader you are studying
- Go backstage and read **interviews** with **famous authors** and **actors**
- Discuss your favourite Readers at the **Book Corner Club**

Visit www.macmillanenglish.com/readers to find out more!